LORD
TEACH ME TO
PRAY
WORKBOOK

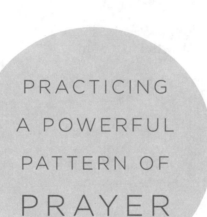

PRACTICING
A POWERFUL
PATTERN OF
PRAYER

KAY ARTHUR

LifeWay Press®
Nashville, Tennessee

Published by LifeWay Press®
© 2007 Kay Arthur

ISBN 1-4158-5321-5
Item 005035558

This book is the text for course CG-1233 in the subject area PRAYER in the Christian Growth Study Plan.

Dewey Decimal Classification Number: 248.32

Subject Heading: PRAYER

Material in this resource is adapted from the book *Lord, Teach Me to Pray in 28 Days*; Copyright © 2001 by Kay Arthur; Published by Harvest House Publishers; Eugene, Oregon 97402. Used by permission.

Unless otherwise noted, Scripture quotations are taken from the New American Standard Bible®, Copyright © 1960, 1962, 1963, 1968, 1971, 1972, 1973, 1975, 1977, 1995 by the Lockman Foundation. Used by permission. *(www.lockman.org)*

To order additional copies of this resource: WRITE LifeWay Church Resources Customer Service; One LifeWay Plaza; Nashville, TN 37234-0113; FAX order to (615) 251-5933; PHONE 1-800-458-2772; E-MAIL to *orderentry@lifeway.com*; ORDER ONLINE at *www.lifeway.com*; or visit the LifeWay Christian Store serving you.

Printed in the United States of America

Leadership and Adult Publishing
LifeWay Church Resources
One LifeWay Plaza
Nashville, TN 37234-0175

Contents

About the Author

In the late 1960s, a missionary couple suffered medical problems and returned home to Chattanooga. Little did they know that God had a greater field of ministry than Mexico for them. Jack Arthur became station manager for a Christian radio station, and Kay Arthur started a Bible study for teenagers in their living room. By 1970, youth were meeting in a barn they had cleaned out and patched up themselves.

Soon adults were coming, too. It became obvious that an expanded ministry center was needed. That's when Jack left his radio career and became President and leader of this flourishing new organization. Today, Precept Ministries International (*www.precept. org*) reaches around the world into 149 countries with studies in 69 languages ministering to children, teens, and adults.

Through the many ministries of Precept—including their daily radio and television program "Precepts for Life," Kay Arthur has touched millions of lives. A well-known conference speaker and author of more than 100 books and Bible studies, she has a unique ability to reach people in an exciting, effective way—teaching them how to discover truth for themselves so truth changes their lives and equips them to be used to advance God's kingdom.

Her authority comes from the Word of God, which she continues to study zealously; her compassion stems from a life that has been touched by deep tragedy as well as great triumph; and her practicality springs from an openness of character.

Amy Summers, a frequent contributor to adult Bible study and discipleship resources, wrote the leader guide. Amy lives with her family in Arden, North Carolina.

About This Study

This workbook study grows out of a fresh update of Kay's popular book *Lord, Teach Me to Pray in 28 Days* (Harvest House). You will treasure getting to know Kay but, more importantly, developing or strengthening your relationship with our Heavenly Father through prayer and Bible study.

If you're uncertain how to pray or wish you could "do better," that's OK! You're in this study to learn how to pray, and you will! Thankfully, Jesus gave His disciples the perfect pattern for prayer, which we know as the Lord's Prayer. Always drawing from His Word, Kay provides intensely practical insights to help you know *how* to pray, *what* to pray, and *what to expect* when you do pray.

You can do this study on your own, but you will benefit from the prayers and support of a small group that is committed to this monthlong journey together. Each group session offers a time to build relationships, discuss the home study just completed, view video teaching from Kay, make personal application, and engage in prayer as a group. Just as you will benefit from the group's support, so can you help someone else develop a prayer life that is vital and powerful.

Each week, between sessions, you have the opportunity to unpack Bible truths through home study. Five days of readings and a "Weekender" feature will help you keep prayer as a daily discipline. Try to make it a priority to do all of the personal learning activities, which are designed to help you to make application to your life and be better able to study the Bible for yourself.

The more time you can commit, the more you will benefit. If possible, try to do home study at the same time and place as part of your daily quiet time. As you do, you will find your prayer life becoming more consistent, effective, and powerful as you communicate with and hear from Him in faith.

Features in your workbook include:
- An overview and goals for each week's home study
- Five days of home study for each week, with Bible teaching, personal learning activities, and an "It's Time to Pray" closure
- A "Weekender" feature that gives you two activities and an opportunity to journal what you have experienced other days
- Video listening guides to help you take notes on Kay's video teachings (pp. 8-9, 34-35, 62-63, 90-91, and 114-115).

Each of the five group sessions is designed for approximately 1½ hours but can be adapted to meet the needs of your small group. Sessions may be held in either a church or a home setting. Be sensitive to using this study as an opportunity for outreach.

If you will be facilitating this study, you will find leader helps in the back of this book (pp. 116-125), as well as in the leader kit (available separately, ISBN 1-4158-3212-9).

Introduction | **Before You Begin**

Are you hurting, beloved? Is the pain running deep? And when I call you *beloved*, do you wonder if you really are loved by anyone, even God? Or maybe right now it's not pain you are facing but doubt, confusion, or stress. Perhaps you're so pressured, so burdened, and so weighed down that you wonder how you are going to make it.

> The news is bad,
>
> > the situation difficult,
> >
> > > the crisis overwhelming,
> > >
> > > > the insecurity debilitating,
> > > >
> > > > > the decision-making process scary.

In any given day you can find yourself concerned about any or all of the following: yourself, your husband (having one, not having one), children (wishing, wanting, having, wishing you didn't), your friends, your finances. The future. The past. The present.

> What are you going to do?
>
> How are you going to make it?
>
> Where are you going to turn?

Your answer is found in the Word of God and in prayer, in casting all your cares on Him because He cares for you. That is what this study is all about, beloved: learning to pray God's way, according to His Word. It is about learning how to talk to God about anything and everything. Or to put it in words that resonate with our spirit, prayer is about communion with God.

I am so excited about what we are going to learn and the incredible difference it will make in your life and in your relationship with the sovereign ruler of the universe. In just four short weeks we are going to learn God's basic precepts on prayer—principles that will give you a biblical understanding of prayer.

Well over a half million people have done the study *Lord, Teach Me to Pray in 28 Days* because it works. Likewise, what you learn in this study, dear child of God, will be yours to put into practice for a lifetime, just as Jesus intended when He taught His own disciples how to pray.

SESSION 1 • YOU ARE GOD'S PRECIOUS CREATION

God is holy and He created all things.

It was God's _____ to create you.

All things have been created through Him, and all things have been created for Him. (See Col. 1:16.)

"Therefore we also have as our ambition, whether at home or absent, to be please to Him" (2 Cor. 5:9).

God has given us a book of prayer.

1. You were created for His pleasure.

2. God has given you a Book, the Bible . It is our textbook, and it also is our prayer book .

   Paul said, "You received the Word of God for what it really is: the word of God" (1 Thess. 2:13).

   The Bible
   • is _____
   • _____ ____ _____ in you
   • is _____ _____
   • can be your book of prayer.

There is a way to pray.

We can learn from His instructions regarding the tabernacle.

Prayer is _____ God, _____ to God, developing a _____ with God.

There is a _____ ___ _____ a holy God.

_____ is holy and _____ are to be holy.

You will learn to approach God as holy.

NOTES

WEEK 1
LEARNING
TO PRAY
GOD'S WAY

Goals for the week

- DISCOVER the truth about prayer by learning what Jesus taught in the Lord's Prayer

- UNDERSTAND how and why prayer is a relationship

- OVERVIEW the ingredients of effective prayer

- LEARN how to "hallow" our Father's name in worship

- BEGIN to practice the Lord's Prayer as a powerful pattern for today

The relationship of all relationships is grown and deepened through the Word of God and prayer, by communicating with the Creator of heaven and earth. In this study you're not only going to see for yourself what the Bible teaches about God's way to pray, you're also going to have the opportunity to put it into practice. What a life-impacting adventure awaits us as a reward for earnestly crying out, "Lord, teach me to pray"! Here is where you'll be going this first week. I will be going there with you too, as I hold you close in my prayers.

DAY 1: Faith Is a Relationship

DAY 2: Prayer Keeps Us Connected

DAY 3: Always Go to the Expert

DAY 4: Come to the Father

DAY 5: Prayer Begins with Worship

DAY 1 | Faith Is a Relationship

Christianity is not a religion; it is a relationship between you and God. This relationship is "Christ in you" as Colossians 1:27 tells us and "you in Christ," as the Ephesians letter so strongly emphasizes in its first three chapters. It takes into account all the issues and more that I touched on in the Introduction to this study.

A healthy, strong, and vital relationship is based on communication: speaking, listening, and understanding. This is why when the pressures of leadership over the affairs of the early church became too much, the twelve apostles knew they had to do something.

Seeing what they did will help us too, so take a moment and open your Bible to Acts 6. In this study I'll be asking you to read a lot from your own Bible so you can make notes and look back at what God is teaching you.

> **Read the first four verses of Acts 6 and list two things to which these early church leaders determined to devote themselves.**

1. _take care of Stephanie_   1. Prayer
2. _cook for the family_   2. Bible

Now then, let's pause for a moment and reflect on our priorities as well. It was the very busyness of life, the pressures of ministry, that caused the Twelve to stop and reflect on what was important. In the same way, we who are also in the midst of incredibly busy lives and ministry to others need to periodically stop and evaluate our priorities. Otherwise we too can miss or neglect the essentials.

> **Let me ask you, What are your top two priorities for every day? Not that you always get them done, but what are your "These are what I am determined to do day in and day out" hopes? Be honest in your answer, for God meets us in our objective honesty. Writing out your priorities is helpful as well.**

1. _take care of Stephanie_
2. _cook for the family_

The Twelve knew that prayer and the ministry of the Word were absolutely vital. They told the congregation: "It is not desirable for us to neglect the word of God in order to serve tables" (Acts 6:2). They were building the church, and

● SUGGESTION BOX

May I make a suggestion? Every time you come across any reference to prayer in your Bible, consider color coding that reference! This is what I (and many other people) do, and it helps so much. Color coding is a learning device that Precept Ministries International has been using for decades.

Choose a color or a symbol (or both) for prayer and mark your Bible every time you come across a reference to prayer. I mark every reference to prayer by drawing a symbol like this ∁ ⌐ in purple and then coloring the word in pink. Another possibility is to draw—over the word or its synonym (words like *request*)—an arrow that points upward ↗.

If you will mark every reference to prayer as you do this study and as you read through your Bible book by book, you will be awed by what you learn. And you also will be able to quickly see all the places where God speaks about prayer.

By the way, I color code all references to the Word of God by drawing an open Bible like this ⌒ in purple and then coloring it green. You may want to mark the references to the word in your Bible, just as you are marking references to prayer.

One last suggestion: You might want to keep your own Journal of Bible Truths in which you list what you learn about various topics such as prayer. This discipline helps you develop a biblical understanding of prayer and becomes your plumb line for measuring the truthfulness of all you hear about prayer.

the church had to be built on the solid foundation of truth. To neglect the Word of God would be a disaster.

Do we understand what they meant when they spoke of the "ministry of the word" in Acts 6:4? Let's make sure we know.

Jesus gave a clear definition of "the word" on His way to the garden of Gethsemane, where He was betrayed and arrested. Let's see what Jesus prayed on behalf of the disciples and all who would believe in Him … which, dear one, includes you!

In His time of crisis, what did Jesus desire for you and me? You can find the answer in John 17:17. (*Of course, I'd like for you to read more of Jesus' prayer to His Father, in verses 1-17, so you can see the context—so vital in handling the Word of God accurately—but if you're in a rush, I understand.*)

Read verse 17 in your Bible and record what the verse says.

_____

_____

Someone has said that prayer and the Word are like two wings of a bird: Both are necessary if the bird is to fly. And both are necessary for us if we are going to soar in our relationship with our Heavenly Father. Just like the apostles, we must give ourselves first and foremost to prayer and to the ministry of the Word. Such priority makes all the difference in the world in the vitality of your relationship with God, beloved. As you discovered in John 17:17, God's Word sanctifies us, sets us apart from the world, for Him. Never forget that God's Word—from the first verse of Genesis to the last verse in Revelation—is pure truth! You can trust it completely, dear one.

> Let's look at another verse that shows us the interlocking of prayer and the Word. Read John 15:7 in your Bible, and in one simple sentence write what you observed from this verse about the relationship of the Word and prayer.

> _____

> _____

> By the way, if you were to mark all references to prayer in your Bible, what synonym for prayer would you mark in this verse?

> _____

Finally, let's look at 1 John 5:13-15 together. Because these verses contain such precious promises, the passage is printed for you so you won't miss a one.

> Read these verses aloud, underlining or highlighting every use of "you," "we," and "us." Then read the passage a second time and mark every reference to prayer. While the word _pray_ is not to be found, there is a synonym.

> 13 _These things I have written to you who believe in the name of the Son of God, so that you may know that you have eternal life._
> 14 _This is the confidence which we have before Him, that, if we ask anything according to His will, He hears us._
> 15 _And if we know that He hears us in whatever we ask, we know that we have the requests which we have asked from Him._

> Now look at every place you underlined "you," "we," and "us" and list every truth you learned from marking the text this way.

> _____

> _____

> _____

> _____

> _____

TWO DISCOVERIES I MADE ARE THAT THE WORD IS:

1. **Written to those who believe in Jesus (v. 13)**

2. **Written so they know they have eternal life (v. 13)**

What did you learn about prayer, or asking, from these verses? The answer is right there in the text. Just look where you marked the word "ask," and write down what you observe.

_____

_____

Now, reason with me: If you want God to hear you and to provide what you ask, then you need to ask according to His will. And how are you going to know His will, beloved? By listening to—knowing—His Word!

God speaks in His Word, and we are to listen. We speak in prayer and God listens. Awesome! Doesn't this truth make you want to give yourself to prayer and to the Word?

IT'S TIME TO PRAY

This daily feature gives you a wonderful opportunity to hear from God and to speak to Him in prayer, to record your thoughts, and to write how He is speaking to you. If you are like me, you will find yourself wanting more time with Him every day.

So what is your prayer today in light of what you've learned? Make it short and simple. Write it here and look back later to see how He answers your prayers.

Oh, God, I _____

_____

_____

_____

_____

_____

_____

DAY 2 | **Prayer Keeps Us Connected**

As we discovered together yesterday, Christianity is a relationship and good communication is part of healthy relationships. In any relationship it is essential to listen, hear, and understand one another. Communication begins with God. He is the initiator of our salvation, and He does that by getting the good news of the gospel to us through His Word or through His people.

The Good News of God

The gospel or good news is defined in 1 Corinthians 15:1-8. Stop and read this passage in your Bible now. Briefly condensed, the good news according to the Scriptures is:

> *Jesus died for our sins and was buried (vv. 3-4). He rose again on the third day and was seen by many (vv. 4-8).*

It's awesome, isn't it? Let's think about His good news for a few minutes. God sent His Son, His only begotten Son who was born of a virgin (and therefore without the sin that every human has at birth) to die for our sins. Your sins, precious one.

When Jesus was crucified, God took your sins, my sins—the sins of the whole world—and placed them on Jesus so that He might become sin for us and we would have His righteousness (2 Cor. 5:21)! Stand in wonder, beloved, at the love of God that would cause the one and only true God to give His sinless Son so that you and I might have eternal life. "God demonstrates His own love toward us, in that while we were yet sinners, Christ died for us" (Rom. 5:8).

What is the proof of eternal life? It is the second point of the gospel: God raised Jesus Christ from the dead, never to die again. The wages or payment for sin is death (Rom. 6:23). Because a sinless Jesus satisfied God's holiness and paid our debt in full, those who believe in Jesus pass from death to life.

If we are true children of God, death will be like going to sleep and waking up in the presence of God Almighty. It is coming home! Living in His presence forever and ever! Never to die a second death, which is the lake of fire (Rev. 20:6,14)! Oh, it is time to talk to God, beloved (are you realizing you can talk to Him *anytime*?) and to say, "Hallelujah! Praise be to God for so great a salvation."

Oh, precious one, do you have forgiveness of sins; do you have Jesus? They go together! Do you believe He is the Son of God, the only Savior? Have you received Him as *your* Lord, *your* God, *your* Savior?

Look at John 1:12. What is God's promise?

We are children of God
We have to submit to Him

Are you God's child? How do you know? What is the proof of your salvation?

_____

_____

If you are not sure, then ask God during this study—even today—to bring you into His forever family. And when He does, may I suggest you write down the date? I was saved at age 29 on July 16, 1963 when I moved from a religion to a relationship. *(I know you are going to figure out my age. Just know I don't feel over 50!)* My changed life (I was a mess) is the evidence of my salvation (2 Cor. 5:17). But I love knowing the date when I was born again (John 3:1-18).[1]

Now then, look at one more thing in 1 Corinthians 15:1-2. When we hear, receive, and stand in this glorious gospel, we are saved—and we hold fast to that salvation. Endurance is evidence of your salvation. May I suggest you read these verses in your Bible and underline the verbs you just read: *received, stand, saved, hold fast.* (If you have a different translation, look for words with these meanings.) Standing firm is a valuable truth that you don't want to lightly pass over.

God's Word Is Truth

When God communicates with humanity, we hear truth—and we either accept it or reject it. But what we or anyone else thinks about the Word of God doesn't change what it is: the very words of God Himself. According to 2 Timothy 3:16 and 2 Peter 1:21, God's Word was inspired or *"God-breathed"* (the Greek word is *theopneustos*) through human scribes so that holy men of God spoke and wrote as they were inspired by the Spirit of God. According to the Bible itself, the Bible is God's Word and it is truth, God's communication to humankind.

Let's review. What, then, is prayer?

Prayer is _____

_____

What role is prayer to take in our lives? How important should it be? How important is prayer to you at this time in your life?

_____

_____

_____

How Often Are We to Pray?

Let's think about this question pragmatically. Every day, it seems, we need to make countless decisions, seek wisdom, locate resources, mend relationships, and communicate love and appreciation.

While the aspects of our daily living may be found in the Word of God in principle, they are not there necessarily in practical detail. Therefore, beloved, we need to talk with and listen to our Heavenly Father. This is prayer. But how often? And when?

Look up 1 Thessalonians 5:17 in your Bible and answer that question from the Word of God.

I am to pray _____

Now does that mean I am to be on my knees in a specific place doing nothing but praying? For heaven's sake, no! Note I said, "for heaven's sake." We must be about our Father's business, and that requires us getting into the world and not only offering others the Word of truth but also showing them by our lives how life is to be lived out in circumstances just like theirs!

What does it mean, then, to pray without ceasing? It means to stay in communication with God, to talk to your Father about everything. When we live like this, we show our dependence on Him and the value we place on His wisdom and leadership in our lives.

Surely you have noticed people walking around with little things in their ears that are not earrings. Those ear pieces tuned to cell phones tend to make people sometimes look at you with glazed eyes. Having an earpiece in place doesn't mean the person is always talking; however, he or she can be connected at a moment's notice.

When you see those earphone connections, let them remind you, beloved, to stay connected with God—to not only talk to Him about everything but also to tell Him throughout the day how much you love Him, need Him, appreciate Him, and depend on Him. To pray without ceasing is to stay connected!

Following Jesus' Example

When Jesus was with the disciples on earth, no cell phones reminded them to pray. However, Jesus—God in man—was our living example of how God intended for us to live when He initially created Adam in His image.

Those who became Jesus' disciples not only heard His teaching on the importance of prayer, they also saw it in His life. After Jesus prayed in a certain place, one of His disciples said to Him, "Lord, teach us to pray" (Luke 11:1). Three instances of Jesus' praying chronologically precede Luke 11:1, our key verse for today. (By the way, Luke is our chronological Gospel.)

Look up the following verses in your Bible and again mark the references to prayer. Then list what you learned.

When you observe a verse, ask the 5 W's and an H: *who, what, when, where, why,* and *how.* In these verses you are looking for the *who* (Jesus), *what* He prayed about or *what* happened when He prayed, *when* He prayed, *where* He prayed, *why* He prayed, and *how* He prayed.

All of these questions won't necessarily be answered, but you don't want to miss the ones that are! Get in the practice, beloved, of carefully observing the text when you study it. Never add to the Scriptures—even in your imagination. God tells you everything He wants you to know.

Luke 3:21-22 _____

_____

Luke 5:16 _____

_____

Luke 6:12-13 _____

_____

Luke 11:1 _____

_____

"Lord, teach us to pray"—you and I would have asked for the same thing, wouldn't we? Jesus' disciples needed to know, and so do we. So here it is: a study of Jesus' response to His disciples when they said, "Lord, teach us to pray," and He replied, "'When you pray, say…'" (Luke 11:1-2).

IT'S TIME TO PRAY

Dear one, if you received Jesus today, then thank Him for the gift of eternal life. Share that decision with someone who can help you grow in Christ. Just think, now you belong to God's forever family. You may want to record the date of your decision here:

_____

DAY 3 | **Always Go to the Expert**

"Lord, teach us to pray" (Luke 11:1). Oh, what wonderful words those are to me! They show me prayer is a skill that can and must be learned. And if prayer is a skill, then it is something I can develop with time and practice.

Now then, my friend, before we go any further may I ask you: What are your current feelings about your prayer life, your communication with God?

Write some words that describe where you are when it comes to prayer. What are your frustrations? Doubts? Desires? Fears? Are you just learning to approach God in prayer? Spill it all out to God. It's good to put your hopes and fears into words.

_____

_____

_____

I think sometimes we feel so inadequate, weak, powerless, and overwhelmed when we hear of the faith and prayer life of others. It's easy to feel that way when we read about giants of faith in the Bible such as the prophet Elijah. Imagine praying and having the very heavens turn off the spigot for three years and six months and then praying again and watching the sky pour rain and the earth produce its fruit (Jas. 5:17-18)! Whew!

"I Could Never Pray Like That!"

We're inspired but at the same time we think, *I could never pray like that.* So we become defeated before we ever start. Or we compare ourselves with others. We read of saints who spent hours, days, or nights in prayer, and we cannot even pray for 10, 20, or 30 minutes. We feel we will never make it, so we give up before we ever begin.

But you *can* develop a meaningful prayer life! God makes certain we know that "Elijah was a man with a nature like ours" (Jas. 5:17). Just know that it will come little by little, growing with your increasing knowledge of God's Word and understanding of God's will. It will come with application, with time, with experience—with the doing of it.

The disciples knew this, and so they began where we must begin if we are ever to learn—with a hunger to be taught. They had seen Jesus praying (Luke 11:1), and they knew that He understood how to pray. They had a hunger to know how to pray, so they went to the expert.

"BY PRAYER WE HOLD THE HAND THAT HOLDS THE DESTINY OF THE EARTH."

ANDREW MURRAY

That is where you and I are also going, beloved of God: to the expert, the Lord Jesus Christ, the Word of God. In the context of Luke 11, Jesus answered the disciples' request by giving them what we call *the Lord's Prayer*. This same prayer is recorded in even greater detail in Matthew 6. Therefore, take a moment and read Matthew 6:5-13.

As you read these verses, you will notice that I am having you read more than what we call *the Lord's Prayer* (vv. 9-13). I am doing this because it is important to read Scripture in context. God doesn't speak in isolated phrases that are unrelated to one another. Nor do we usually—unless we are a frustrated parent! Therefore, whenever you study the Word of God, check out the context. Remember this: *Context rules over all interpretation.*

As you read Matthew 6:5-13, mark every reference to prayer. *(If you don't want to mark your Bible right now, why don't you use a pencil? Just remember it is not a sin to mark or write in your Bible. The Bible is your textbook for life. God wants you to study and know it, and marking the text helps you do that.)*

Now, let's do some observation. Let's see what the Word of God says in Matthew 6:5-13 about praying. List below what you learn simply from marking the references to praying—nothing more. Number your insights.

_____

_____

_____

As you read, you came across the word *hypocrites* (v. 5). A hypocrite is like a person who wears a mask. He is two-faced, saying one thing but meaning another. A hypocrite pretends to be something other than what he or she is!

When Jesus gave the disciples this prayer, did He mean they were simply to say the prayer over and over? Was He saying that the way to pray was to use these words? Look at the context. Immediately before Jesus said, "'Pray, then, in this way'" (Matt. 6:9, italics added), He said, "'When you are praying, do not use meaningless repetition'" (Matt. 6:7). It is obvious that the Lord's Prayer was not meant to be a prayer said by rote, simply repeated over and over. This is what I did Sunday after Sunday for 29 years. I recited the words in a meaningless way. But then, wow! After I got saved, the words took on a whole new meaning to me. What I was saying and what I was asking for were awesome, relevant, and weighty!

A Way to Pray

Then the day came when I discovered something else about the Lord's Prayer. I realized when Jesus said, "'Pray in this way,'" He was giving them a way to pray, not a prayer to pray. *(Not that it is wrong to pray the Lord's Prayer!)* Jesus was using the same manner of instruction that the rabbis (teachers) of His time used. He was teaching the disciples an index sentence of the various topics to be covered in prayer.

Index prayers were a collection of brief sentences, each of which suggested a subject for prayer. Remember, books in biblical times were not plentiful for the average person. They were all copied by hand. The printing press wasn't invented until the 1400s! So teachers used learning devices or techniques such as index sentences. Memorizing the index sentence would prompt what someone was to remember or do.

The Ingredients of Effective Prayer

I believe, as do others, that the Lord's Prayer states for us in topical form the ingredients necessary for effective prayer. Nowhere else in God's Word did the disciples say to Jesus, "Teach us to pray" (Luke 11:1). Nowhere else did Jesus directly say, "Pray, then, *in this way*" (Matt. 6:9, italics added).

Therefore, to pray according to the index or the topical outline of the Lord's Prayer is to pray—to communicate—in a way that is pleasing to the One to whom you are talking, the sovereign ruler of the universe.

Let's take a look now at what is called *the Lord's Prayer* and see the topic of each index sentence. Your assignment is to: (1) pray, asking God to help you hear and understand what He is teaching in these verses—the issue of each sentence that you are to cover in prayer; and (2) write next to each sentence the topic or issue with which it deals.

Keep your answer as short as possible; one word will do, but you can write more if you want. This is for you to think through, beloved. It is so important to think. When you became God's child, He gave you the mind of Christ (1 Cor. 2:16). Use it! Do not be anxious about being clever or eloquent in your titles. Don't think you have to use alliteration, making all the titles begin with the same letter. That is not the point. By now you know there is nothing eloquent about my writing or speech (if you've heard me on radio, television, or in person), yet God uses them. So relax. Let God give you His insight.

I have numbered the sentences for you. You can record the theme of each on the line next to it.

1. Our Father who is in heaven,
   Hallowed be Your name.   _____

2. Your kingdom come.   _____

3. Your will be done,
   On earth as it is in heaven.   _____

4. Give us this day our daily bread.   _____

5. And forgive us our debts, as we also
   have forgiven our debtors.   _____

6. And do not lead us into temptation,
   but deliver us from evil.   _____

7. For Yours is the kingdom and the
   power and the glory forever.   _____
   Amen. Matthew 6:9-13

Great! You have prayerfully thought this through, and I am proud of you. We'll talk more about your answers tomorrow. Just know that my heart is so filled with love for you. I am so proud of you for studying God's Word.

Now, how about accepting a holy challenge? Would you covenant before God that without fail you will set aside a specific time for prayer each day for the next 26 days? Tell Him you are coming to Him as a learner. Tell Him you have no hope if He doesn't help you!

Sometimes it helps solidify your commitment when you sign your name and the date of your commitment here.

_____

IT'S TIME TO PRAY

Now, follow Jesus' example, beloved child of God. Get alone with the Father and know that He is waiting and eager to have time alone with you.

Talk to your Father about one of the topics in the Lord's Prayer that has touched you where you are right now. Maybe you need deliverance from temptation, petition for a need, or forgiveness in a relationship.

You get the point, don't you? Make time to get alone and pray, "and your Father who sees what is done in secret will reward you" (Matt. 6:6). Write what is on your heart. Talk with Him about what you have learned.

_____

_____

_____

_____

DAY 4 | **Come to the Father**

Just think what it would be like to have every principle of prayer condensed into several simple sentences so you could remember them easily. No matter where you find yourself, you could then recall those sentences and use them to talk with your Heavenly Father in a meaningful and vital way.

Oh, beloved, once you learn to pray—and you know it is *His* way, *His* will that you pray—then you will discover there is absolutely nothing sweeter than knowing you have touched the hem of His garment in prayer. It's healing! It's renewing! It brings a quietness, a stillness. It brings peace, a calming confidence that flows over your soul like the balm of Gilead.

Because God wants our communion with Him to be sweet, effective, and powerful, He taught us through His Son how we are to pray. As we saw yesterday, the Lord's Prayer is a collection of index sentences, covering every element of prayer. Therefore, when you follow sentence by sentence, precept by precept, principle by principle, you will find yourself covering every possible aspect of prayer.

The Lord's Prayer is the true pattern for all prayer. Oh, what a treasure our Lord gave to His disciples, and us, when they said, "Lord, teach us to pray."

Today we will begin looking sentence by sentence at this pattern for prayer. As we do, I am going to take you to other Scriptures that will amplify, illuminate, illustrate, or substantiate each particular precept or understanding.

Now, I do not want you to merely be a passive reader of truth. You need to actively participate in what you are learning. Therefore, when you are asked to do something, please do it. I say that beseechingly. This is not busy work—it is essential work. The Word of God and the Spirit of God are schooling you. If you'll do what I ask and not just read, I guarantee you will learn.

Each activity will help you seal truth to your heart and teach you to pray by the very doing of it! I know it works. We've taught all levels of inductive study from 40-Minute Bible studies with no required homework to Precept Upon Precept Bible studies that take five hours a week. People have done it for years, and it is transforming—transforming because it is the Word of God, and His words are spirit and life, the very bread by which we live. Now, let's dig in.

The Topics of Prayer

Yesterday you looked at the topics covered in the Lord's Prayer as recorded in Matthew 6:9-13. For the sake of continuity, let me give you how I summarized the topics covered by the index sentences.

1. **Our Father who is in heaven, Hallowed be Your name.**   *Worship*

2. **Your kingdom come.**   *Allegiance*

3. **Your will be done, On earth as it is in heaven.**   *Submission*

4. **Give us this day our daily bread.**   *Petition & Provision*

5. **And forgive us our debts, as we also have forgiven our debtors.**   *Confession & Forgiveness*

6. **And do not lead us into temptation, but deliver us from evil.**   *Watchfulness & Deliverance*

7. **For Yours is the kingdom and the power and the glory forever. Amen. Matthew 6:9-13**   *Worship*

The last sentence (7) is not in the earliest manuscripts but was added later. However, you can see that it brings prayer full circle as it begins and ends with the worship of God.

Although we may have worded our categories differently, I think we can all agree that the Lord's Prayer covers these basic and all-encompassing topics. Everything God's Word says on the subject of prayer can be aligned under one of these index sentences. Great, isn't it!

To pray according to the pattern of the Lord's Prayer is to cover every topic of prayer. It's a thorough work of prayer. But does this mean that every time you pray you cover all the topics—all the bases, so to speak?

Do I Pray "This Way" Every Time I Pray?

If you study all the times people communicated with God in prayer, you'll see that the answer to this question is no. Therefore, be careful not to impose something on yourself or others that God does not impose. As you may know, sometimes all we can do is cry "Oh Lord!" or "Help, Father." It seems I am constantly asking God to find something I've misplaced. When that happens, believe me I don't cover all seven topics. However, you will find me worshiping Him in the process. "Father, You're omniscient. You know where it is." Then when it is found, it's worship again: "Oh thank You, Father, thank You."

If you use the Lord's Prayer for what it is, the way to pray, it will not only keep you balanced when it comes to prayer but it will also be a wonderful guide, a road map of prayer so to speak. Often when I am sitting in an airport, riding in the car with my husband, or lying in bed trying to wake up or go to sleep, I start praying sentence by sentence …

- lingering on each topic as the Lord leads, bringing those things on my heart to Him;
- beginning with worship but then turning to kingdom matters and submission to the will of God;
- calling out to the Father on behalf of my children and grandchildren, our staff, our trainers, or our students, that each might keep the kingdom before them and will to do His will.

This, beloved, is the practicality of knowing and using the Lord's Prayer. As the Master Teacher, Jesus covered it all and in a way that is memorable. In fact, it's meant to be memorized.

A Prayer to Be Memorized

If you do not know this prayer, you really need to memorize it.

Read aloud Matthew 6:9-13 three times in a row every day (or sing it if you prefer). Reading it out loud is the key.

Now write Matthew 6:9-13 on index cards; then put them where you will be able to read them at strategic times during the day.

You have just practiced two effective ways to memorize Scripture; you can use these with other verses you want to commit to memory. By the way, when you memorize Scripture, may I suggest you use word-for-word translation (for example, King James Version, New American Standard Bible, English Standard Version) rather than a paraphrase? I value God's every word!

Do I Pray to God or to Jesus?

"Our Father." This, beloved, is where all true prayer begins. It begins with God the Father, and it ends with God the Father. True prayer is nothing more and nothing less than communion with the Father. Whether you are involved in worship, intercession, petition, or thanksgiving, it is all directed to God the Father.

You often hear people pray, "Dear Jesus" or "Jesus." Yet should we direct our prayers to the Father or to the Son? Jesus tells us to pray "Our Father." Yes, we come in the name of Jesus, for He is the One who gives us access to God through His death, burial, and resurrection; but it is all to bring us ultimately to the Father.

Now, then, one final word: When you come to God the Father in prayer, think about why you are coming to Him, what you believe about Him, and what is necessary on your part.

Read Hebrews 11:6 aloud. It is printed for you below.

> *"Without faith it is impossible to please Him, for he who comes to God must believe that He is and that He is a rewarder of those who seek Him."*

Now read this verse again out loud and answer these questions.

• **What are you to believe when you come to God in prayer?**

_____

_____

• **Why are you coming to Him?**

_____

_____

• **How are you to come to Him?**

_____

_____

It takes faith not only to please God but also to come to God the Father. And what is faith? It is defined in Hebrews 11:1: "Faith is the *assurance* of things hoped for, the *conviction* of things not seen" (italics added).

Prayer begins by communicating with a God who, although you have never seen Him, is there. Those who come to Him must believe **He is!** He is what? He is God! And that He is a rewarder of those who seek Him. You come; He responds and rewards. Awesome! You have a God who exists and who cares; that is why you come to Him. "What then shall we say to these things? If God is for us, who is against us? He who did not spare His own Son, but delivered Him over for us all, how will He not also with Him [Jesus] freely give us all things?" (Rom. 8:31-32).

Whoa! Don't go any further. Read those two verses again. Think about them. Surely they tell you how precious you are to your Heavenly Father. Worship Him. Thank Him for being there for you and for being able to give you whatever you need. Worship is an essential ingredient to faith.

Oh, beloved, do you see it? Jesus wants you to realize you are not coming to some remote, untouchable, indifferent Sovereign. You are coming to a Father—our Father—a Father with children, a Father who loves, who cares, and who longs to have fellowship with His children, with you.

PRAYER IS A DISCIPLINE THAT WHEN EXERCISED WILL GIVE YOU A GREATER INTIMACY WITH YOUR FATHER BUT WHEN NEGLECTED WILL MAKE YOU FEEL DISTANCED FROM HIM.

IT'S TIME TO PRAY

Take a few minutes to talk to God just as a child would talk to his or her own earthly father.

"But, Kay," you may say, "my father never talked to me, never cared for me, so how can I talk to God as a father?" Even though you may have had that kind of father, didn't you long for one who was loving, affectionate, caring, and accessible? Well, here He is, waiting for you to talk to Him.

Spill it all out ... aloud. Tell God what you think about Him as a Father. Tell Him your fears, your hopes, your hesitations, your expectations. Tell Him what you long for in a relationship.

Remember the personal issues I asked you about in the introduction to this study? Lay those before Him if they are applicable. Then ask God what He longs for ... and listen carefully.

Take note of what comes to your mind, giving Him time to speak. (If the thoughts are from God they will be in accord with the Word of God and the character of God. If they are not, then they are not from God.) Write those things you want to remember, things He brought to your mind, or what you cried out for.

_____

_____

_____

_____

DAY 5 | **Prayer Begins with Worship**

First and foremost, prayer is about God. Like the Bible, like creation itself, prayer begins with God! How incredibly awesome—God, our Father! You are not alone; you are a part of the family of God. Right from the beginning, Jesus makes that fact clear with the words, "'Our Father.'"

These words also tell us that prayer belongs to those who are children of God. Prayer is a family privilege. When we came to know God through Jesus Christ, God "rescued us from the domain of darkness, and transferred us to the kingdom of His beloved Son" (Col. 1:13).

You're Part of His "Forever Family"

Consequently, "you are no longer strangers and aliens, but you are fellow citizens with the saints, and are of God's household'" (Eph. 2:19). Jesus told us that "'whoever does the will of My Father who is in heaven, he is My brother and sister and mother" (Matt. 12:50). We are no longer "of your father the devil" (John 8:44). Ephesians 2 has some wonderful reminders: we are no longer "children of wrath" (v. 3), no longer "the sons of disobedience" (v. 2), no longer "dead in our transgressions" (v. 5). Rather, we have been "made ... alive together with Christ" (v. 5), "a dwelling of God in the Spirit" (v. 22).

You are coming to a Father who loves you and who desires your highest good. "If you then, being evil, know how to give good gifts to your children, how much more will your Father who is in heaven give what is good to those who ask Him!" (Matt. 7:11).

Prayer Begins with Worship

The very fact that you pray is to worship God. Why? Because you are acknowledging that God exists and that you need Him. Prayer demonstrates that you value God for who He is, the one true God! The One totally set apart from man. The One who is other than man, more than man. He is God, the first and the last. Jehovah—LORD—the self-existent One (Gen. 2:4; Ex. 3:13-15; 6:3). There is no God besides Him (Isa. 44:6). Thus, beloved, when you come to God in prayer, you are coming to One greater and mightier than yourself, One whose memorial name to all generations is "I AM."

The word *worship* carries the connotation of bowing, prostrating one's self before another. To worship God is to bow before Him, prostrate yourself before His person, acknowledge His worth, and give Him the honor and reverence due Him. A good way to remember the English meaning of *worship* is to think of looking at someone's worth. When we worship God, we rightly acknowledge God's worth, who He is and what He is able to do.

● WORSHIP

Worship becomes the basis of everything that follows in prayer: *allegiance* to His kingdom, *submission* to His will because He is, after all, God! Such prayer is *petitioning* Him for what you need because you are acknowledging that the earth and everything it contains is the Lord's.

Because He is holy and has given us His commandments and precepts for life, we are accountable to Him. Thus, we are to *confess* when we go against His holy Word and must seek His *forgiveness*: "Against You, You only, I have sinned and done what is evil in Your sight" (Ps. 51:4). God is the One who knows our temptations and the Tempter. In a spirit of *vigilance* we seek God's *deliverance* from the Evil One. All of this brings us again to *worship*, for His is the kingdom, the power, and the glory, forever.

When you think about it, for prayer to begin and end with worship of the One who is in heaven—above the earth, above all—is only logical. The Lord who has "established His throne in the heavens" and whose "sovereignty rules over all" (Ps. 103:19) is able to do "according to His will in the host of heaven and among the inhabitants of earth" (Dan. 4:35). Worship correctly prepares us for all that follows in prayer.

Hallow (Not Hollow) His Name

Hallow is the word translated from *hagiazo* and comes from *hagios*—to make holy, to set apart, to make a person or thing the opposite of common. To hallow His name is to reverence it by believing God is who His Word says He is and that He will always be and always do what He says.

God's name represents who God is. It reveals His character and His attributes. The psalmist wrote that "You have magnified Your word according to all Your name" (Ps. 138:2). "According to" could be translated "together with." In other words, God's Word stands because God's name stands.

Do you remember God's commandment "You shall not take the name of the LORD your God in vain, for the LORD will not leave him unpunished who takes His name in vain" (Ex. 20:7)? *Vain* means "empty, worthless—hollow" rather than "hallowed."

The opposite of taking the Lord's name in vain is hallowing it! We take God's name in vain when we disbelieve, deny, or distort the truth about God. As I said earlier, God's names testify to His character. If you hallow His name, then you acknowledge and respect who He is and behave accordingly. When you and I refuse to believe God is who He says He is and will do what He says He will do, then we demean and defame Him. We hollow His name.

That is something to think about, isn't it? Many who would never think of taking the Lord's name in vain by swearing or by speaking it in a casual way still desecrate His name when they doubt, deny, or defame His character.

Knowing God by Name

Now let me share some of the names of God so you may *hallow*—revere, respect—Him according to His worth.

> **Read "The Names of God" chart carefully, paying attention to the various names of God and what they mean. When you have time, you will benefit greatly by looking up the Scripture references where these names are used (perhaps writing them in the front or back of your Bible). Then you'll see the context in which God reveals each particular aspect of His character.**

THE NAMES OF GOD

Name	Scripture	Means or Shows God as
Elohim	Genesis 1:1	Creator
El Elyon	Genesis 14:18-20	The Most High (Sovereign)
Jehovah-Tsidkenu	Jeremiah 23:6	The Lord our Righteousness
Jehovah-Jireh	Genesis 22:14	The Lord will provide
Jehovah-Roi	Psalm 23:1	The Lord is my Shepherd
Jehovah-Shalom	Judges 6:24	The Lord is peace
Jehovah-Nissi	Exodus 17:15	The Lord is my Banner
Jehovah-Rophe	Exodus 15:26	The Lord who heals
Jehovah-Shammah	Ezekiel 48:35	The Lord is there
Jehovah-Sabaoth	1 Samuel 1:3-11	The Lord of hosts

* The Hebrew word Jehovah is often rendered Yahweh.

Years ago, when studying the Lord's Prayer I thought, *Father, How can we fully hallow Your name if we don't know it?* Thus, the popular book *Lord, I Want to Know You* was born. It has been life-changing for hundreds of thousands because they learned who their God is and how to call on His name. The stories of what God has done when individuals made His Name their strong tower are miraculous—I'll share a couple with you in my teaching! They will thrill and encourage you to call on the name of the Lord in the day of trouble.

The Place of Worship in Prayer

Romans 15:4 tells us that what "was written in earlier times was written for our instruction." So there's much we can learn about prayer from Old Testament saints.

Look up the highlighted references in your Bible. Under each one (after I put it into context) note how the prayer begins—with worship, petition, and so forth. Then record how the individuals involved worshiped God, what they said or acknowledged about Him. Don't forget to mark any words for prayer.

ISAIAH 37:14-20 • Second Kings 18:13-37 tells that Sennacherib, the king of Assyria, was threatening to destroy Jerusalem if King Hezekiah would not surrender. Its condensed form is found in Isaiah 37. It was a day of distress, rebuke, and rejection for Hezekiah, and he felt he had no strength to do anything about it (v. 3). Ever had a day like that? Read verses 14-20 and learn from him.

How prayer begins   **How God is worshiped**

_____   _____

2 CHRONICLES 20:3-19 • It was another bad day in the land of Israel. Jehoshaphat, the king of Judah, had three armies coming against him, and he was afraid.

How prayer begins   **How God is worshiped**

_____   _____

ACTS 4:23-31 • Peter and John healed a man and caused a stir (3:1-10). By preaching Jesus, they upset religious leaders who ordered them to quit preaching in Jesus' name (4:18).

How prayer begins   **How God is worshiped**

_____   _____

Now, beloved, stop and think about a day when you dealt with distress, rebuke, rejection, threats, or enemies. If it happens again, how can you apply what you have learned today?

_____

_____

In the three prayers you looked at, God's name was hallowed. Now it is time to do the same, dear worshiper of God.

IT'S TIME TO PRAY

"Holy and awesome is His name" (Ps. 111:9). The Bible tells us "The name of the Lord is a strong tower; the righteous runs into it and is safe" (Prov. 18:10). Choose one of the names from the chart that deals with where you are today; then call on that name, telling your Heavenly Father you want to hallow His name by believing and living accordingly.

1. The story of how Kay met our loving God, who freed her to serve Him with her whole heart, is available by contacting Precept Ministries International (www.precept.org or 1-800-763-8280).

WEEKENDER

I am so proud of you for doing your homework, beloved. It is essential for you to discover truth for yourself. Thank you for disciplining yourself for the purpose of godliness. You will never regret it.

Learning to pray God's way according to His Word becomes a pattern when we spend time with Him every day. Each week this Weekender page helps you include time with Him in your weekend schedule, As you refresh from the week, don't miss a day in the Word and in communication with the Father.

List some ways you are learning to hallow God's name.

_____

_____

_____

_____

_____

How has God been answering your prayers this week?

_____

_____

_____

_____

_____

SESSION 2 • LEARNING TO PRAY GOD'S WAY

The Lord's Prayer is a prayer of _____ _____.

Index Sentence 1: "Our Father who is in heaven, Hallowed be Your name."

"Our Father who is in heaven"

Prayer allows you to _____ to the One who holds the world in His hands.

Prayer has its _Source_ in God.

Prayer _begins_ with God as the sovereign ruler of the universe.

When we come to God in prayer, we come to God who is in heaven.

We pray because _God_ _uses_ _us_ _here_ to help Him accomplish His work. This is the mystery of prayer.

You are never more _powerful_ than when you are on your knees.

"Hallowed be Your name"

We are to _reverence_ His name.

When I am in trouble, I can _run_ to the name of the Lord.

He is Jehovah-Jireh: The LORD will _provide_

In prayer we are holding the hand of the God whose name is greater than any other name.

Prayer is based on _intimacy_ with the Father.

El-Roi: You are a _God who sees_

"The name of the LORD is a strong tower;
The righteous runs into it and is safe."
Proverbs 18:10

NOTES

WEEK 2
IT'S ALL
ABOUT HIM

Goals for the week

- EXPLORE what it means to worship God in truth

- UNDERSTAND how sin impacts your prayer life

- EXAMINE the vital roles of allegiance and submission in prayer

- IDENTIFY how kingdom work is accomplished through prayer

- PRACTICE the Lord's Prayer as a powerful pattern for today

When Jesus began to teach the disciples how to pray, He knew the necessity of their hearts being aligned with the heart of God. Redeemed men and women have an awesome call on their lives—that of kingdom business. But how many of us really understand the role of prayer in accomplishing our calling from God?

My prayer is that during this next week especially, God will show you how significant your prayers are and that, consequently, you will be about the Father's kingdom business.

DAY 1: Rehearsing the Character of God

DAY 2: Eagerly Awaiting Him

DAY 3: For the Sake of the Kingdom

DAY 4: A Heart Attitude for Today

DAY 5: Our Greatest Example

DAY 1 | Rehearsing the Character of God

Prayer begins with worship—focusing on God, rehearsing truth, calling on God whom we know and trust. It is sad that many of us are so busy, so stressed, so enamored and entangled with the world that we really don't know God as He wants us to know Him. And this has ramifications for our prayer life.

Some of us are more familiar with the New Testament than with the Old, but it's in the Old Testament that God introduces Himself, progressively unfolding His person in His names, His character, His commandments, and His ways with people and nations. It is in the Old Testament that we develop our knowledge and understanding of God. Daniel 11:32 assures us that "the people who know their God will display strength and take action" or as the KJV says "shall be strong, and do exploits."

Yet for many in today's world the appeal seems to be for "Bible lite," simplified, not demanding, heavy on application, loaded with good stories, and easy on doctrine and Scripture. Nothing hard, please, or too time consuming. Consequently, when we come to "Our Father who is in heaven, hallowed be Your name," there's not always an abundance of truth in our treasure chest of praise and worship.

Sometimes our thanksgiving, which is part of worship, is lacking as well. How can we "enter His gates with thanksgiving and His courts with praise"? How can we "give thanks to Him" and "bless His name" (Ps. 100:4) if we don't really know and understand Him? How can we speak of "His faithfulness to all generations" (v. 5)?

If we are not at home in the Word, it's difficult to turn to passages where we can rehearse His names, attributes, commandments, and promises, not to mention His dealings with people and nations.

If you are weak in the Word, beloved, you will be weak in prayer. The two go hand in hand. The greatest book on prayer is the Bible. It should be our "book of common prayer."

Our lack of a true biblical knowledge of God can even show in the songs we sing. Think of all the songs you can still sing—even the silly ones you learned from childhood! It is a vivid reminder that music can stay with us.

I believe many of the worship songs we sing repeatedly should be even stronger in biblical content. We need to make certain that we are worshiping in truth and singing choruses, songs, and hymns of biblical substance. Rather than seeking only a stirring of our emotions, we primarily should be concerned about transforming our minds to the mind of Christ. Just think what we could be engrafting in our hearts, minds, and souls if we sang songs of even greater biblical substance.

The doctrine found in the first hymn ever penned by Isaac Watts is a wonderful example. Dissatisfied with the dismal singing at church, Isaac's father challenged him to write his own music. As a 19-year-old, Watts wrote "Behold the Glories of the Lamb" based on the truths of Revelation 5. Isaac's 600-plus hymns have lasted because they are built on eternal truths.

GEORGE MUELLER

Listen to the words of George Mueller, a man who saw mighty answers to prayer as he was led by God to care for orphans without asking for financial support:

"Faith cometh by hearing and hearing by the word of God" (Romans 10:17). We must hear! Listen! Hearken! I must ask myself, "Whom am I listening to? To GOD and His WORD? Or to what people say? Careful reading of the Word of God, combined with meditation on it. In that way we become acquainted with God; His nature, His ways, His will, His loving assurances, His sure promises, His mercies, His everlasting care and His manifold cures. Confidence grows, faith is given and answers are assured."[1]

Behold the glories of the Lamb
Amidst His Father's throne.
Prepare new honors for His name,
And songs before unknown.

Eternal Father, who shall look
Into Thy secret will?
Who but the Son should take that Book
And open every seal?

Now to the Lamb that once was slain
Be endless blessings paid;
Salvation, glory, joy remain
Forever on Thy head.

Thou hast redeemed our soul with
   blood,
Hast set the prisoners free;
Hast made us kings and priests to God,
And we shall reign with Thee.

In Scripture when you find people worshiping the Godhead, you never find them repeating the same phrases over and over, such as, "Praise You, Jesus; praise You, Jesus." How much richer would this chorus be if we expressed what we are praising Him for, singing of His attributes and His glorious works!

Granted, in Isaiah 6 you find the seraphim calling out, "Holy, Holy, Holy, is the LORD of hosts" (Isa. 6:3). However, such a threefold repetition was simply the way of denoting the ultimate of a truth; here it is the holiness of God.

In Matthew 6:7, preceding His teaching on the way to pray, Jesus admonished His disciples not to "use meaningless repetitions as the Gentiles do." Centuries later, John Wesley was used by God in the Great Awakening. Commenting on Jesus' Matthew 6 teaching, Wesley cautioned those he taught with these words, "Do not use abundance of words without any meaning. Say not the same thing over and over again; think not the fruit of your prayers depends on the length of them ... the thing here reproved is not simply the length, any more than the shortness of our prayers; but, length without meaning; speaking much, and meaning little or nothing."[3]

Idol worshipers often worked themselves up through excited and frenzied repetition of a phrase in the worship of their gods; but with the children of God, this was not so! In biblical worship you do not find the use of repetitive phrases; rather, you find worshipers rehearsing the character of God and His ways, reminding Him of His faithfulness and His wonderful promises.

Power in prayer is found in faith. Our worship should be founded—rooted, grounded—in truth, not emotion. Worship should not be based on the fervency of our words or the loudness of our voice, but on the faithfulness of our God. Emotion is natural, but genuine emotion follows truth!

Worshiping God in Truth

Let's turn again to some prayers God has preserved for us in His Word and see what we can learn from others who worshiped God in truth (John 4:24). You do realize, don't you, that Jesus said the Father seeks such people to be His worshipers (v. 23)? Want to fill out a job application?

Let's look at three prayers of worship: Hannah's, Jeremiah's, and Daniel's. If you don't have time for all three, do at least one.

- **Read each of the prayers in your Bible. Don't rush.**
- **Mark the references to prayer (don't forget the synonyms) in your Bible as you have done previously.**
- **Observe how the worshiper uses his or her knowledge of God in prayer, and see what you can learn.**
- **Under each Scripture reference, list what you learn about God—such as truths you want to remember about the One you are to worship in truth.**

1 Samuel 2:1-10

_____

_____

_____

Jeremiah 32:16-25

_____

_____

_____

Daniel 2:19-23

_____

_____

_____

IT'S TIME TO PRAY

Take what you learned about God from the prayer(s) you just studied and write a prayer, poem, or song to worship God.

_____

_____

_____

Day 2 | **Eagerly Awaiting Him**

Our second index sentence, "Your (God's) kingdom come," is potent in its brevity. What does it mean? Why is it a topic for prayer? What is covered in this category of prayer? For a while I linked "Your will be done, on earth as it is in heaven" with "Your kingdom come." I couldn't see why these two sentences had to be separated. It took meditation to gain understanding, and with it came the feeling that for many in the body of Christ this is a truth greatly lacking.

"Your kingdom come" is a confirmation in prayer of our allegiance to the sovereign rule of the kingdom of God above all else—of our desire for God's visible rule upon the earth. The Jews, the people of Israel, awaited it. After the death and resurrection of Jesus Christ, Gentile believers joined them in watchful anticipation. But I had missed it!

Although I was raised in church for the first 29 years of my life, I never knew Jesus would literally return to earth and set up His kingdom. I had a Bible but was blind to this truth because His Book bored me. Basically, I only heard snippets of the Word on Sunday mornings as portions of the Gospels and other Scriptures were read from both sides of the platform in front of the altar.

I recited the Apostle's Creed and the Lord's Prayer every Sunday without fail with the rest of the congregation, and yet I never knew Jesus was coming again. I was in the church and loved it. I taught Sunday School, was active in the youth group, loved the church picnics and outings, and dated one of the clergy who was filling in for the summer; but I never knew that Jesus would return to rule and reign on planet earth!

Nor did I hear that I had to be born again, to believe on Jesus and personally receive Him, acknowledging Him as the Son of God and the only way to the Father. I had been baptized as a infant and confirmed at the age of 13, and that was supposed to do it! I had never heard of a literal heaven, and I most certainly did not know of a literal hell.

> **Once I had no idea what I was saying when I prayed, "Your kingdom come." What about you? How I wish we could curl up in our pajamas and discuss this issue face-to-face as women. When you hear "Your kingdom come," what comes to mind?**

_____

_____

> **Do you think _worship_ and _allegiance_ are synonymous? Give the reason for your answer.**

_____

_____

I just finished 55 television teaching programs in Israel on the Gospel of Matthew. What an experience—to teach Matthew in the very land where Jesus lived and taught its truths. It was an incredible experience for our entire team.

From his first words, Matthew established the fact that Jesus is the Messiah, the son of Abraham, the son of David, the One who will sit on the throne of David and whose kingdom will have no end. Then he began to tell us what His kingdom is all about as John the Baptist came preaching, "Repent, for the kingdom of heaven is at hand" (Matt. 3:2). Jesus followed John, preaching, going throughout all Galilee proclaiming the gospel of the kingdom.

In the Sermon on the Mount Jesus told them to whom the kingdom of heaven belongs. And in teaching them how to pray, Jesus told us to pray that the Father's kingdom would come and that His will would be done on earth as it is done in heaven.

I could go on and on walking us through Matthew, reading of Christ's return, the setting up of His throne on earth, the drinking again of the fruit of the vine with His faithful disciples in the kingdom until we come to the final words of the Gospel, Jesus' commission to the eleven. (Eleven because one defected. Judas had not given his allegiance to Jesus.)

Read Jesus' closing words again, beloved, and this time color or put a box around *authority*.

> *"And Jesus came up and spoke to them, saying, 'All authority has been given to Me in heaven and on earth. Go therefore and make disciples of all the nations, baptizing them in the name of the Father and the Son and the Holy Spirit, teaching them to observe all that I commanded you; and lo, I am with you always, even to the end of the age'"* (Matt. 28:18-20).

Let's observe what you marked.

• **Whose authority?** _____

• **How did He get it?** _____

• **How extensive is that authority? Where does it reach or what does it cover?** _____

_____

• **How much authority does He have?** _____

_____

• **What is the basis of Jesus' command to the disciples? (Hint: When you see a "therefore," find out what it's there for.)**

_____

_____

The kingdom of God is all about His authority over us, over all mankind. It's about knowing there is a God—only One—and it is not you, it is not me, it is not us. It is God and because He is God, I am to give my total allegiance to Him and to no other.

Do you know people who acknowledge the worship of God yet do not seem fully aligned with His kingdom and its preeminence? What things appear to take priority in their lives?

_____

_____

Over what do those things seem to take precedence?

_____

_____

How is this priority manifested in the way they live?

_____

_____

I know people who stand and extol God for who He is. Yet, even though they know and confess Him properly, their actual allegiance is to the furtherance of their ambitions, their welfare, their creature comforts and luxuries, their education and advancement, their legalistic set of do's and don'ts, … their whatever, or so it often seems. I know people who say, "I know I should study God's Word more," or "I know I should witness," or "I know I should give more" or "I know I should be more involved in His work, but …"

But what? What are they really saying? Record your thoughts.

_____

_____

I think in reality they are saying, "But my first allegiance is not to God." Think about it. And think about where you are, beloved. Now, your next question may be, like mine, "But doesn't allegiance fit right in with submission to His will when we pray, 'Your will be done'?" Yes, the two do go together. But true, complete, absolute submission to God's will is born only out of undivided, absolute allegiance to His kingdom.

Unfortunately, many of us—even those who attend church and profess Christianity or a belief in God—have fallen flat on our faces in the mud of the world! Instead of living in total obedience, unwavering allegiance to His kingdom and His reign as King in our lives, we are double-minded, desiring the best of both worlds, forgetting that "our citizenship is in heaven, from which also we eagerly wait for a Savior, the Lord Jesus Christ" (Phil. 3:20).

We are not eagerly awaiting Him because we have entangled ourselves in the affairs of everyday life and have forgotten we are to please the one who enlisted us as soldiers (see 2 Tim. 2:4). Too often our allegiances are to money and what it provides, to position and its prestige, to things and their pleasures, and even to "churchianity" and its works. Notice I say _churchianity_, not _Christianity_. Churchianity puts people first; church is about them and their desires. Christianity puts Christ in His rightful place as head of the church.

Don't we often only give lip service to God? We want only enough of Christianity to get us to heaven, only enough to get our prayers answered and the benefits of healing and prosperity. We do not want to give total allegiance to His kingdom because it calls us to a cross. We do not want His kingdom to come today, tomorrow, or even within a few years because, like Demas, we love this present world more (2 Tim. 4:10). Is this right or is it wrong? Does any of it describe you?

I don't mean to sound harsh, beloved, but as I write this, truth is "in my heart … like a burning fire shut up in my bones" (Jer. 20:9). Oh, how my heart grieves as I see multitudes who name His name yet who have not given Him their total allegiance. Oh, how my heart grieves when the Spirit of God shows me incidents when I failed to give my absolute, total, unwavering allegiance to Him, the Lord God of all heaven and earth. Do you realize that God calls us to discern? Study Matthew 7 carefully, and you will see that our fruit—our doing or not doing of the Word—bears witness to our allegiance.

When people have time for everything except a personal, diligent study of God's Word, we know they are not approved unto God (2 Tim. 2:15). They know much about the world but little about God! Why? Because they have time for the things of this life but not time to study God's Word. They refuse to believe that "man shall not live on bread alone, but on every word that proceeds out of the mouth of God" (Matt. 4:4). Communion with God through His Word and prayer is essential to the fruitful life that will hasten the coming of His kingdom.

Filling in the words of the first two index sentences, following our example of the One who tells us how to pray, is good review for your memorization of the Lord's Prayer.

"Our _Father_ _who_ _is_ _in_ _heaven_,
Hallowed _be_ _Your_ _name_.
Your _Kingdom_ come."

Now read Matthew 4:8-10 in your Bible. Mark each reference to the Devil. I use a red pitchfork like this ⚔. Don't miss the pronouns as you read.

• What was the Devil offering Jesus in this passage?

the devil showed him the world

• What did the Devil want from Jesus in exchange?

want Jesus to worship him

• How does Jesus' response line up with the first two index sentences of the Lord's Prayer?

_Get out of here Satan
You must worship the Lord +
serve only him_

Now let's think. Although this was Jesus and the Devil, we know we have an adversary, the Devil. How would the Devil tempt us in a similar way?

_temp us to believe that
money + power is more important
than the truth (Bible)_

• What should be our answer?

_____

_____

_____

When Jesus calls men and women to Himself, for what kind of allegiance does He ask? Carefully read these Scriptures and (1) circle or color every reference to those to whom Jesus is speaking; and (2) underline or use a different color to show everything the person is told to do.

34 *"He summoned the crowd with His disciples, and said to them, 'If anyone wishes to come after Me, he must deny himself, and take up his cross and follow Me.*
35 *For whoever wishes to save his life will lose it, but whoever loses his life for My sake and the gospel's will save it' "* (Mark 8:34-35).

25 *"Now great multitudes were going along with Him; and He turned and said to them,*

26 *'If anyone comes to Me, and does not hate his own father and mother and wife and children and brothers and sisters, yes, and even his own life, he cannot be My disciple.*

27 *Whoever does not carry his own cross and come after Me cannot be My disciple.'" (Luke 14:25-27).*

37 *"'He who loves father or mother more than Me is not worthy of Me; and he who loves son or daughter more than Me is not worthy of Me.*

38 *And he who does not take his cross and follow after Me is not worthy of Me.*

39 *He who has found his life will lose it, and he who has lost his life for My sake will find it'" (Matt. 10:37-39).*

"'Seek first His kingdom and His righteousness, and all these things will be added to you'" (Matt. 6:33).

Anything less that denying yourself, taking up your cross and following Him (Mark 8:34), hating your family and even your own life, seeking His kingdom first—anything less is divided allegiance. Anything less will not allow you to honestly pray, "Your kingdom come." Therefore, when you pray, "Your kingdom come," examine yourself to see whether anything in your heart is keeping you from undivided allegiance to the coming of His kingdom.

IT'S TIME TO PRAY

Oh, beloved, why don't you go to our Father and ask Him to show you anything that is dividing or dissipating your allegiance to His kingdom? Write it down.

_____

_____

Then, if you feel that you might slip back, confess this to your husband or to a close and faithful friend in the Lord, and together seek God in prayer. Ask them out of love to hold you account-able for, "Two are better than one because they have a good return for their labor. For if either of them falls, the one will lift up his companion. But woe to the one who falls when there is not another to lift him up" (Eccl. 4:9-10).

DAY 3 | For the Sake of the Kingdom

As the itinerant evangelist made his way to the sixth village on his journey, his heart was filled with joy. It was Christmas. Having seen a number of Chinese come to believe in Jesus, he was anticipating the same success in this village.

"Greetings," I called to a group of villagers. "I am bearer of good news. The ..." A man interrupted me.

"We have only bad news here," he said irritably. "A couple has just had their baby stolen." (Kidnapping and selling babies is not uncommon in China.)

As the evangelist shared their sorrow he said, "I know someone who can help you—God. Let me pray to Him on your behalf." There was no reaction on their sad faces. "Yet," he writes, "I went into prayer anyway, feeling very uncomfortable; 'Dear Father, many years ago at this same time of year You sent a child into the world and rescued us all. I ask that You bring back this man's child and deliver this village from sadness.'"

Suddenly the young father of the stolen child spoke out, "Shut up and go away. We have prayed to our gods and nothing has happened. Why should yours be any different?"

The people propelled the evangelist from the village. His Christmas joy turned to sorrow. He felt like a total failure as he made his way down the road in a daze of humiliation and tears. Then he remembered Jesus, His commission to go and make disciples, His rejection, and His willingness to suffer in order to accomplish the will of His Father.

Though frightened, for the sake of the kingdom of God, the evangelist turned and walked slowly back to a village. His heart wouldn't let him do anything else. As the afternoon sun began its descent, he heard the cry of a baby from the shaft of a well. The baby's face was blue, its little bottom uncovered. Then he understood. When the captors discovered the baby was a girl, she was abandoned in the well. Girls were of no value. Those who purchased kidnapped babies only wanted boys.

When the people of the village saw him carrying the baby, they came running—the mother among them. The smile on her face seemed almost holy. "Come and warm yourself by our fire," the father said. "Who was that God you prayed to?"

Allegiance to the kingdom of God brought the evangelist back, and God opened their hearts to believe.

Furthering the Kingdom of God

When you and I pray "Your kingdom come," we are asking God to further His kingdom. Yes, to bring His visible rule upon the earth but also to bring it to the hearts of men now, in these last days that began with the first coming of the Son of God (Heb. 1:2). The gospel comes individually before it comes globally.

Write what Jesus said in Matthew 24:14 about the gospel of the kingdom. (I color code references to God's kingdom like this ♛.)

_____

_____

_____

Read Matthew 24:30 and 25:31 and record what you learn. The "end" references the end of the present age brought about when Jesus Christ ...

_____

_____

_____

By the way, I mark every reference to the second coming of Jesus Christ with a cloud like this: ☁. Then I color the center yellow and the rest, light blue.

What does Revelation 14:6-7 tell us about the proclamation of the gospel? As you write your answer below, notice who is going to do what, for whom, and when it will happen.

_____

_____

_____

If this is going to happen, then what is our responsibility? Who is to get out the good news of the gospel until then? Do you remember Jesus' words as recorded in Matthew 28:19-20? We looked at them earlier.

> "Go therefore and make disciples of all the nations, baptizing them in the name of the Father and the Son and the Holy Spirit, teaching them to observe all that I commanded you; and lo, I am with you always, even to the end of the age."

Read them again and double underline "make disciples," the sentence's main verb. "Go" (literally "as you are going"), "baptizing," and "teaching" are participles supporting the main verb.

So what is our task as believers in Jesus Christ?

_____

_____

Making disciples begins, beloved, with sharing the gospel. And what is the gospel? Can you remember what we learned in our first week of study? List below the two main points we saw in 1 Corinthians 15. You need to know and remember them if you are going to proclaim them!

1. _____

2. _____

Debtors to the Gospel

Just before Jesus ascended to heaven, His disciples asked Him a question. Read Acts 1:6-8 and answer the following questions:

• What were the disciples asking Jesus?

_____

• What was His answer?

_____

• According to verse 8, what were the disciples to be?

_____

• Where were they to do this?

_____

Jesus will restore the kingdom to Israel when He returns as King of kings and sits on David's throne. But until that time the followers of Jesus Christ have a mission and commission. Why? Because men are born in sin and will perish if they do not receive forgiveness of their sins by believing in Jesus Christ. Never forget that. There is salvation in no other (Acts 4:12). Romans 10 makes it clear they cannot believe in someone of whom they have never heard. They must hear; therefore, we must share. This is why Paul saw himself as a debtor to

"Thy kingdom come"

"There is no ministry that will bring more power and blessing than the habit of believing, definite, and persistent prayer for the progress of Christ's kingdom, for the needs and work of His church, for His ministers and servants, and especially for the evangelization of the world and the vast neglected myriads who know not how to pray for themselves."
— A. B. Simpson

"THY KINGDOM COME" is where …
- you remember that through Jesus God "rescued us from the domain of darkness, and transferred us to the kingdom of His beloved Son" (Col.1:13).
- you fall before your Father who is in heaven, having seen His holiness and say, "Here am I, Lord, send me."
- in intercessory prayer you plead for your husband, your children, your loved ones, your neighbors, your nation, the world—His sheep who have yet to hear His voice and come to Him that they might have eternal life (John 10:27-29).
- you "'beseech the Lord of the harvest to send out workers into His harvest'" (Matt. 9:38).
- you see the fields that are white—over-ripe—to harvest, and like Jesus you say, "My food is to do the will of Him who sent Me and to accomplish His work" (John 4:34) and begin by praying, "Thy kingdom come in China, in Zambia, in Iran, in _____!" Wars are grievous, beloved, but God often uses them to bring people to their knees and then give them the gospel.
- you pray, as commanded, "for the peace of Jerusalem" for there will never be permanent peace until the Prince of Peace returns and "the Lord will be king over all the earth" (Ps. 122:6; Zech. 14:9).

the gospel. In Romans 1:16 Paul wrote that the gospel is the power of God for salvation to all who believe, to the Jew first and then the Greek (all who are not Jews). And we are debtors!

Prayer Is Kingdom Work

When we pray "Your (or "Thy") kingdom come" we are about kingdom work— getting the gospel to the lost. The kingdom cannot come until His body is complete, until the last of His sheep is brought into the fold, for He will not lose one of His (John 10). "The Lord is not slow about His promise [to return and set up His kingdom], as some count slowness, but is patient toward you, not wishing for any to perish but for all to come to repentance" (2 Pet. 3:9). Therefore, when you pray for the coming of His kingdom, you are "hastening the coming of the day of God" (v. 12).

The world is on God's heart; if this is the way we are to pray, the world is to be on our hearts as well. It's on your knees, precious one, that you make your commitment, bowing before Him, honoring your Father as your God, and making yourself available as His ambassador wherever He sends you. It is on your knees that you water the soil of men's hearts through prayer so the ground is ready to receive the seed of His word.

Would you get on your knees now and simply say to God, "Father, my allegiance is to You alone. May Your kingdom come"?

Jack and I just received a leather edition of *Adrianisms—The Wit and Wisdom of Adrian Rogers* from our dear friends, Bill and Barbara Skelton. Adrian was a pastor at Bellevue Baptist Church in Cordova, Tennessee, for 32 years. He and his wife, Joyce, whom I love and admire, lived passionately for God's kingdom, faithful unto his death. His absolute belief was—and I can hear him now:

> "No matter how faithfully you attend church, how generously you give, how circumspectly you walk, how eloquently you teach, or how beautifully you sing, if you are not endeavoring to bring people to Jesus Christ, you are not right with God."

Is your unwavering allegiance also to the kingdom of God?

IT'S TIME TO PRAY

Read the quote from A. B. Simpson again (p. 50) and be encouraged to pray as you put into practice what you've learned in these first two index—topical—sentences. In preparation for prayer:

• First list several truths you know about your Heavenly Father in respect to the kingdom of God and the gospel of Jesus Christ.

_____

_____

_____

• Then worship Him according to what you know about Him. For instance, you might write that He loves the world so much that He gave His Son. You would then take that truth and pray something like this:

> *Oh Father, I thank You for loving me, for loving people so very much that You sent Your very own Son to earth to die for all mankind. Oh God, thank You, Jehovah-Jireh, for providing Jesus as the sacrifice for my sins and for the sins of the whole world.*

Giving your allegiance to God might sound something like this:

> *Father, I know that I am to share this good news with others, and I am scared. But if you will help me, I will do it. I want to be obedient. And Father, would You go before me by Your Spirit and prepare their hearts? I think especially of my neighbor, Lord. She so desperately needs you. She's hurting so badly.*

From there you might pray for a country, for those sitting in darkness at home and abroad; for those who are suffering illness or abuse; for Muslims, Hindus, Buddhists, and so forth. Pray for those whom God by His Spirit lays on your heart.

As you pray, beloved, pray aloud. Confessing truth and hearing ourselves pray seals and confirms our prayers in our hearts and minds. It also helps keep our thoughts from wandering.

Finally, beloved, pray, "Come, Lord Jesus" (Rev. 22:20). Thy kingdom come.

DAY 4 | A Heart Attitude for Today

"Your will be done, on earth as it is in heaven" follows allegiance to God's kingdom. Our hearts long for the reign of God on the earth, the end of blatant sin, blasphemy, rebellion, and man's inhumanity to man. We long for the earth to be filled with the knowledge of the Lord as the waters cover the sea, for every knee to bow and every tongue to confess Jesus Christ for who He truly is. We cherish the fact that Jerusalem will be a praise in all the earth and all the nations will come to see His glory. Yes, this is our first and rightful thought as we pray, "Your will be done, on earth as it is in heaven."

Yet is this merely a prayer only to be fulfilled when Jesus returns and "the sovereignty, the dominion and the greatness of all the kingdoms under the whole heaven will be given to the people of the saints of the Highest One," when "all the dominions will serve and obey Him" (Dan. 7:27)?

A Prayer for the Present

"Your will be done" is not only a prayer to pray as we wait only for the coming kingdom; it is a heart attitude of *present* submission to the *present* sovereignty and will of the Father. If you are going to pray correctly *and* have your prayers answered by God, you must be willing to do His will now while the entire world lies in the power of the Evil One (1 John 5:19), opposing God's truth and reign.

What is God's will, His work, first and foremost? Read the following verses and box or color every occurrence of the words *work* and *will*. Then underline what the work or will of God is.

Jesus answered and said to them, "'This is the work of God, that you believe in Him whom He has sent'" (John 6:29).

38 *"'I have come down from heaven, not to do My own will, but the will of Him who sent Me.*

39 *This is the will of Him who sent Me, that of all that He has given Me I lose nothing, but raise it up on the last day.*

40 *For this is the will of My Father, that everyone who beholds the Son and believes in Him will have eternal life, and I Myself will raise him up on the last day'"* (John 6:38-40).

Now, beloved, read the following three passages and circle every occurrence of *believe*, *believes*, and *believing*. Then underline what happens to those who believe or don't believe.

44 *"Jesus cried out and said, 'He who believes in Me, does not believe in Me but in Him who sent Me.*

45 *He who sees Me sees the One who sent Me.*

46 *I have come as Light into the world, so that everyone who believes in Me will not remain in darkness'"* (John 12:44-46).

8 *"'He [speaking of the Spirit of God], when He comes, will convict the world concerning sin and righteousness and judgment;*

9 *concerning sin, because they do not believe in Me'"* (John 16:8-9).

"These have been written so that you may believe that Jesus is the Christ, the Son of God; and that believing you may have life in His name" (John 20:31).

The work of God is that you believe on the Lord Jesus Christ whom God has sent (see John 6:40). He is God incarnate. *Incarnate* means "in the flesh." Therefore, Jesus is God in the flesh (John 1:1-2,14). In other words, the Father's will is that you believe Jesus Christ who has come in the flesh, born of a virgin (Matt. 1:20-25) and without sin (2 Cor. 5:21) is God—I AM. Not to believe this truth is to die in your sins (John 8:24). Those who do not believe in the Lord Jesus Christ are sinning (John 16:9), going against the will of God and, therefore, remain dead in trespasses and sins (Eph. 2:1). The wrath of God abides on them (John 3:36), for "there is salvation in no one else; for there is no other name under heaven that has been given among men by which we must be saved" (Acts 4:12).

Read this paragraph again. If it contains anything you do not believe, cross it out in the paragraph. Then go to the "address" of that truth in the Bible—book, chapter, and verse—and cross it out of your Bible. Write why you don't believe it.

_____

_____

The Lord's Prayer is God's way for believers to pray. Jesus' first words confirm this: "Our Father." We know from John 8:44 and others that there are only two fathers and each human being belongs to one of them: the Devil or God.

As you have seen, salvation is submission to truth. Believing. Aligning yourself under it. The Devil is a liar and the father of lies who abides not in the truth, although at times he will speak truth as Matthew 4:6 demonstrates. (See John 8:44.) God is truth; Jesus is the truth (John 14:6). To believe that Jesus is God is to acknowledge His position and rights as God. To recognize Him as Savior is to see that only this God-man can save you from your sins. Jesus took on flesh and blood so that He might taste death for every person (Heb. 2:9).

Reason with Me Now

And what is the root of all sin? Is it not independence? Is it not self having its own way? Isaiah 53:6 says that like sheep we have turned each "to his own way." If you look up each of the verses that actually define sin, you discover that each verse shows to one degree or another that we have willfully chosen to break the law, to not believe, to choose *our* path rather than God's.

One of the evidences of salvation is a willingness to submit to God—to recognize that because He is God and you are His creation, you are to submit to Him. So before we pursue this attitude of submission in respect to prayer, let's look at the relationship of submission and salvation.

In your Bible observe Matthew 7:21-27 carefully, and answer these questions (watch for the word "will"):

• **Who is going to enter the kingdom of heaven?**

_____

• **Whose house is going to stand the storms and why?**

_____

• **How did Jesus describe those He said He never knew? What were they doing?**

_____

• **According to verse 22, does what they did show they were saved and going to enter heaven?**

_____

• Why were they not going to enter the kingdom of heaven?

_____

_____

• Whose house fell and why? _____

_____

• Where is submission is all this?

_____

• With which of these two groups do you identify?_____

_____

Look up John 9:31 in your Bible and write it below.

_____

_____

• Based on this verse, who does God not hear? _____

_____

_____

• Who does God hear and why? _____

_____

_____

• What does this have to do with submission?_____

_____

_____

If you and I are not willing to say to God in prayer, "Your will be done, on earth as it is in heaven," can we expect our prayers to be answered? Whew! That is something to really stop and think about it, isn't it?

IT'S TIME TO PRAY

Oh dear one, are you still in your sins, or are you a worshiper of God who longs to do the will of the Father? Only the latter has access to God in prayer. Therefore, you better settle this with God if you are not a true worshiper of His. Beloved, may I suggest that you spend some time in prayer talking to the Father about His will? List any area you have not submitted to the will of God.

_____

_____

_____

May I make one more suggestion? If you can, get flat on your face before God on the floor and spread out your hands, so that your body takes the form of a cross. In that position pray, "Thy will be done on earth—now, in me—as it is in heaven."

DAY 5 | **Our Greatest Example**

The One who teaches us to pray, "Your will be done on earth, as it is in heaven" is the One who is our greatest example of submission to the will of God. Of course as I say that, if you are familiar with the Word of God, the Spirit of God takes your mind immediately to the garden of Gethsemane. Let's go there. While each Gospel records what happened, Matthew elaborated on the prayers of our Savior at that time.

As you read the Matthew 26:36-44 ...

- Mark or color in a distinctive color every reference to prayer.
- Put a circle around every reference to time along with a squiggly line. I draw an old fashioned clock over references to time in my Bible and then put a squiggly line under the entire reference to time. For example, I mark "a second time" like this. ☺
- Put a box around those words Jesus used to refer to the will of God, or color them yellow.

36 "*Then Jesus came with them to a place called Gethsemane, and said to His disciples, 'Sit here while I go over there and pray.'*

37 *And He took with Him Peter and the two sons of Zebedee, and began to be grieved and distressed.*

38 *Then He said to them, 'My soul is deeply grieved, to the point of death; remain here and keep watch with Me.'*

39 *And He went a little beyond them, and fell on His face and prayed, saying, 'My Father, if it is possible, let this cup pass from Me; yet not as I will, but as You will.'*

40 *And He came to the disciples and found them sleeping, and said to Peter, 'So, you men could not keep watch with Me for one hour?*

41 *Keep watching and praying that you may not enter into temptation; the spirit is willing, but the flesh is weak.'*

42 *He went away again a second time and prayed, saying, 'My Father, if this cannot pass away unless I drink it, Your will be done.'*

43 *Again He came and found them sleeping, for their eyes were heavy.*

44 *And He left them again, and went away and prayed a third time, saying the same thing once more*" (Matt. 26:36-44).

Read all of the following questions before you answer them, as your answers can overlap. It's OK if they do. The purpose of the activity is to make sure you observe the text accurately and see exactly what God has recorded for us through Matthew.

What do you learn from marking the references to prayer?

_____

_____

What did Jesus pray?

_____

_____

What do you learn from marking the references to time?

_____

_____

Do you think this was easy for Jesus? After all, He is God and He knew what was going to happen.

Before you answer, look at what Luke told us in Luke 22:41-44. Write your discovery in the blanks provided.

_____

_____

Now, look at three other Scriptures that chronologically lead up to Luke 22. Read them carefully and record what they tell you about Jesus' knowledge of and submission to the will of God.

> *"The Son of Man has come to seek and to save that which was lost"* (Luke 19:10).

_____

_____

_____

> *"'Now My soul has become troubled; and what shall I say, Father, save Me from this hour? But for this purpose I came to this hour. Father, glorify Your name'"* (John 12:27-28).

_____

_____

_____

> 1 *"Jesus spoke these things; and lifting up His eyes to heaven, He said, 'Father, the hour has come; glorify Your Son, that the Son may glorify You,*
> 2 *even as You gave Him authority over all flesh, that to all whom You have given Him, He may give eternal life.*
> 3 *This is eternal life, that they may know You, the only true God, and Jesus Christ whom You have sent.*
> 4 *I glorified You on the earth, having accomplished the work which You have given Me to do'"* (John 17:1-4).

_____

_____

_____

Jesus knew why He came—to be the Lamb of God who would take away the sins of the world—but the cost to be paid was horrendous: hell! For the first and only time in all of eternity, the Father would forsake His Son because the wages of sin is death and death is separation from God. As we know, He would cry, "MY GOD, MY GOD, WHY HAVE YOU FORSAKEN ME?" (Matt. 27:46). Yet it was the will of God—the corn of wheat would have to die or it would abide alone. Thus He could not say, "Save Me from this hour." It was for this hour that He had come. He had been born to die, and He would not turn back. He would glorify the Father. He would accomplish the work God gave Him to do.

This, beloved, is the One who tells us to pray "Your will be done." Can you see how God progressively brings us to this point in prayer? First, we acknowledge who God is and honor Him accordingly: "Our Father who is in heaven, hallowed be Your name." Then, we give Him our allegiance: "Your kingdom come." And third, we tell Him we want His will to be done here on earth in us as it is done in heaven.

The work of the kingdom is accomplished by our submission and obedience to the will of God. Kingdom work cannot be done apart from doing what God desires. "We are His workmanship, created in Christ Jesus for good works which God prepared beforehand so that we would walk in them" (Eph. 2:10). Oh precious child of God, do you realize this? Do you believe this? Will you pray accordingly? Pause for a few minutes and talk to your Father about the truths I have written and you have studied.

As you surrender yourself to know and do His will, you'll want to pray it for others. I often use Paul's prayer in Colossians 1:9-12.

Let's study it, and then we'll pray. As you read,
- **Mark the references to prayer.**
- **Put a box around the reference to His will.**
- **Color "knowledge" green.**

> 9 *"For this reason also, since the day we heard of it, we have not ceased to pray for you and to ask that you may be filled with the knowledge of His will in all spiritual wisdom and understanding,*
>
> 10 *so that you will walk in a manner worthy of the Lord, to please Him in all respects, bearing fruit in every good work and increasing in the knowledge of God;*
>
> 11 *strengthened with all power, according to His glorious might, for the attaining of all steadfastness and patience; joyously*
>
> 12 *giving thanks to the Father, who has qualified us to share in the inheritance of the saints in Light"* (Col. 1:9-12).

Why did Paul want them to be filled with the knowledge of God's will? Record your thoughts on the next page.

_____

_____

_____

Number the things in verses 10-12 (beginning with *so that you will walk*) that are to be manifest in our lives. For example, I put a circled 1 above *to please*. You continue with 2, 3, and so forth.

10 *so that you will walk in a manner worthy of the Lord, to please* ⑦
    Him in all respects, bearing fruit in every good work and
    increasing in the knowledge of God;
11 *strengthened with all power, according to His glorious might, for*
    the attaining of all steadfastness and patience; joyously
12 *giving thanks to the Father, who has qualified us to share in the*
    inheritance of the saints in Light" (Col. 1:10-12).

IT'S TIME TO PRAY

Today simply pray Colossians 1:9-12 aloud, mentioning the name of the person(s) you want to pray for wherever you see a "you." Do you know what is so valuable about praying Scripture? You are praying according to the Word and will of God. Don't give up ... give God time to work His good work in their lives.

Be like the persistent friend Jesus used as an illustration in Luke 11. Keep on asking and it will be given to you, keep on seeking and you will find, keep on knocking and it will be opened (Luke 11:5-10; Matt. 7:7). "Ask," "seek," and "knock" are all in the present tense in the Greek, which implies continuous or habitual action. Persevere, beloved.

1. George Mueller, "Answers to Prayer" in Armin Gesswein's School of Prayer (Pasadena, CA: International Intercessors, May 1985).

2. Robert J. Morgan, *Then Sings My Soul* (Nashville, TN: Thomas Nelson Publishers, 2003), 30 .

3. "The Sermons of John Wesley" [online] 2006 [cited December 7, 2006]. Available from the Internet: http://new.gbgm-umc.org/umhistory/wesley/sermons/26/

WEEKENDER

Learning to pray God's way according to His Word becomes a pattern when we spend time with Him every day. Each week this Weekender page helps you include time with Him in your week-end schedule. As you refresh from the week, don't miss a day in the Word and in communication with the Father.

What competes for your allegiance to God? Take your list to Him in prayer, and ask Him to change you.

_____

_____

_____

_____

_____

How has God been answering your prayers this week?

_____

_____

_____

_____

_____

IT'S ALL ABOUT HIM

SESSION 3 • IT'S ALL ABOUT HIM

Index Sentence 2: "Your kingdom come."

Index Sentence 3: "Your will be done, on earth as it is in heaven."

If we are going to have our prayers _____ and _____, our allegiance must be to God.

"Now then *let Me alone*" (Ex. 32:10, italics added).

Faith is not faith until it is tested.

"So the Lord *changed His mind*" (Ex. 32:14, italics added).

Do you see the _____ _____ _____ when we give Him our allegiance?

In times of testing, where is your _____ going to be?

> "He [Daniel] continued kneeling on his knees three times a day,
> praying and giving thanks before his God,
> as he had been doing previously" (Dan. 6:10).

Index Sentence 3: "Your will be done, on earth as it is in heaven."

Power begins with _____ to God.

When you walk with God in prayer, when you give your allegiance to Him and submit to Him, you can _____ Him.

This is where you find your _____.

This is where you find your _____.

This is where you find the _____ to go on.

NOTES

WEEK 3
YOU BELONG
TO GOD

Goals for the week

- FOCUS on praying according to God's will

- ACKNOWLEDGE ways God provides for you

- LEARN why dependence on God is necessary and make specific commitments to rely completely on Him

- PRAY the Lord's Prayer as a powerful pattern for today

Beloved, we're dealing with some meaty issues. As you begin to see a change of direction this week in the Lord's Prayer, continue to worship Him for His goodness and provision to you. Be faithful.

DAY 1: Our Prayers Connect Heaven and Earth

DAY 2: His Mosaic of Exquisite Design

DAY 3: A Faith That Soars

DAY 4: Total Dependence on God

DAY 5: The Lord Who Provides

DAY 1 | **Our Prayers Connect Heaven and Earth**

Have you ever finished your prayer time feeling it was useless? I have, and it is so frustrating. After such times my emotions have varied from a feeling of total impotence, to guilt (because of a wandering mind), to a sense of almost despair. I have wondered, *Father, will I ever learn?*

Surely Jesus sensed this would happen to us, for prayer is probably the most disciplined and difficult exercise in the Christian's life. Oh, how I love this God of ours who has truly promised to supply all of our needs … even our need in prayer. How I thank Him for opening my eyes to see what Jesus was doing when He said, "'Pray, then, in this way'" (Matt. 6:9).

It has been so exciting to realize that the Lord's Prayer is an index prayer, a collection of brief sentences, each suggesting a subject of prayer. Now we know *how* to pray. All we have to do is recite one sentence of this prayer at a time, realize what topic or point it covers, and then simply talk to the Father about anything that falls under that particular part of the index. When we finish the first point, we move on to the second.

To go through the entire collection of index sentences is to cover the whole plain of prayer. Or, as G. Campbell Morgan, the prince of expositors, said, "To pray that prayer intelligently is to have nothing else to pray for. It may be broken up, each petition may be taken separately and expressed in other ways, but in itself, it is exclusive and exhaustive."

Oh, beloved, do you see? Memorize the Lord's Prayer and no one can take from you God's way to pray. You will have it for the rest of your life. From the youngest babe in Christ to the most mature saint, here is the way you can pray and know that your prayers are pleasing to God. And it's a form of prayer that will expand as you deepen in your knowledge of and walk with Him.

When you take time to study the Lord's Prayer carefully, you will begin to pick up on a change of direction in the pattern of prayer. Read Matthew 6:9-13 to see if you can discover this change for yourself.

Mark the references to God including "Your" in one color or way.
Highlight the references to "us" and "we" in a different color.

9 *"Pray, then, in this way: 'Our Father who is in heaven,*
   Hallowed be Your name.
10 *'Your kingdom come. Your will be done, On earth as it is in*
   heaven.
11 *'Give us this day our daily bread.*
12 *'And forgive us our debts, as we also have forgiven our debtors.*
13 *'And do not lead us into temptation, but deliver us from evil.*
   For Yours is the kingdom and the power and the glory forever.'"

Prayer connects heaven with earth as you come to your Father at His throne, worshiping Him, giving Him your allegiance, and telling Him of your commitment to His will. As you gain heaven's perspective, you lay all earthly matters and concerns at the feet of your sovereign God.

You probably saw when you marked the references to *God* and *us* that the prayer's pattern changes between verses 10 and 11. The first segment focuses on God and His kingdom, His will. Then in verse 11, having settled these things, you bring the matters of earth to Him, beseeching His help: *give, forgive, lead us not, deliver.* Why? Because His is the kingdom, the power, and the glory, forever and ever. Amen! So be it!

God's will is crucial. Desiring it, here, now. Knowing it. Submitting to it. Romans 12:1-2 tells us how to find God's will. Read aloud these verses, printed for you below, before doing any observations. It's good to hear Scripture. (I like to listen to it on CDs in the mornings as I get dressed for the day.)

> 1 *"Therefore I urge you, brethren, by the mercies of God, to present your bodies a living and holy sacrifice, acceptable to God, which is your spiritual service of worship.*
>
> 2 *And do not be conformed to this world, but be transformed by the renewing of your mind, so that you may prove what the will of God is, that which is good and acceptable and perfect."*

"Therefore" follows the statement that "from Him and through Him and to Him are all things. To Him be the glory forever. Amen" (Rom. 11:36). Because God is the source, means, and end of all things and to Him belongs the glory forever, it is our reasonable service of worship to do what Romans 12:1-2 says: to present ourselves as living sacrifices. Isn't that what we do in prayer when we bow before God, hallow His name, pledge our allegiance to His kingdom, and tell Him we unreservedly submit to His divine will while we live on earth?

How will we know God's will? Read Romans 12:1-2 aloud again. Underline in your Bible every reference to God's will in these verses. Now answer the questions that lead to accurate observation of the text.

• What does the text (especially the parts you've underlined) tell you about God's will? List your insights below.

_____

_____

_____

_____

- **What enables you to prove (to put to the test for the purpose of approval) what God's will is?**

  _____

  _____

- **According to the text, what would keep you from knowing God's will? What are you _not_ to do?**

  _____

  _____

Since God's will is good, acceptable, and perfect, don't you long to be right in the middle of it? I desire to be there with you, beside you, knowing without a shadow of doubt that this is the will of God in Christ Jesus concerning me.

I am a lover of Christian biographies, especially those of men and women of past generations. Next to the Word of God, they are the books that ministered to me most as a new Christian, giving me a vision of what it was like to walk with God, believe Him, obey Him, and do His will no matter the cost.

Among these men is George Mueller (also see p. 38). He lived two centuries ago (1806-1898); yet his life continues to show that God never changes, that He hears and answers prayer. Until he was converted, Mueller was truly chief among sinners. His conversion came when he saw a group of his contemporaries on their knees in prayer.

But let's allow him to tell his own story of how he came to start his orphanages and, for over 60 years, to see God supply the needs of the orphans—sometime daily, sometimes hourly, without telling anyone of the need, but God alone. Let's see what we can learn about prayer and discerning God's will.

> The first and primary object of the Institution was ... that God might be magnified by the fact that the orphans under my care were, and are, provided with all they need only by prayer and faith, without anyone being asked by me or my fellow-laborers, whereby it might be seen that God is FAITHFUL STILL AND HEARS PRAYER STILL.
>
> I never remember in all my Christian course, a period now of sixty-nine years and four months, that I ever SINCERELY AND PATIENTLY sought to know the will of God by the teaching of the Word of God, but I have been ALWAYS directed rightly.
>
> But if honesty of heart and uprightness before God were lacking, or if I did not patiently wait upon God for instruction, or if I preferred the counsel of my fellow men to the declarations of the Word of the living God, I made great mistakes."[1]

Oh, how well I understand. I have made some very unwise decisions—great mistakes—because I did not wait patiently upon the Lord for instruction or I did not diligently seek Him. Once I simply went with my heart and did what was kind and generous but not God's will. Years later I reaped the consequences.

George Mueller applied biblical principles in his decision making. I truly believe they are ones you will want to use. He writes:

1. I seek at the beginning to get my heart into such a state that it has no will of its own in regard to a given matter. Nine-tenths of the difficulties are overcome when our hearts are ready to do the Lord's will, whatever it may be. When one is truly in this state, it is usually but a little way to the knowledge of what His will is.

2. Having done this, I do not leave the result to feeling or simple impression. If so, I make myself liable to great delusions.

3. I seek the will of the Spirit of God through, or in connection with, the Word of God. The Spirit and the Word must be combined. If I look to the Spirit alone without the Word, I lay myself open to great delusions also.

4. Next I take into account providential circumstances. These plainly indicate God's will in connection with His Word and Spirit.

5. I ask God in prayer to reveal His will to me aright.

6. Thus through prayer to God, the study of the Word and reflection, I come to a deliberate judgment according to the best of my ability and knowledge, and if my mind is thus at peace, and continues after two or three petitions, I proceed accordingly. In trivial matters and transactions involving most important issues, I have found this method always effective.[2]

Beloved, aren't you anxious to get on your knees and seek to know God's will?

IT'S TIME TO PRAY

What do you need to know, to understand? In which areas of your life do you need direction? On a separate piece of paper, or perhaps in a journal or even inside your Bible write your questions. Date them.

Then go to the Father and present yourself as a living sacrifice. Tell Him His will is your will. You know it will be good, acceptable, and perfect because that's what the will of God is. Spread your list before the Lord and apply what you've learned today. Stay in His Word; it is your book of prayer.

Day 2 | **His Mosaic of Exquisite Design**

As you titled each index sentence in the Lord's Prayer did you wonder, *But where is intercession on behalf of others? I did not see it in the Lord's Prayer, and surely God wants us to pray for others!*

You are so right. I asked our Father the same question, and He showed me where it was. I got so excited! Maybe you've already seen it, but in case you haven't, let me show you how to find it. It's the rich fruit of observation.

Read through the Lord's Prayer again.

- **Mark every singular personal pronoun:** *I, me, my, mine.*
- **Mark the plural personal pronouns:** *we, our, us.*
- **From memory write the general topic of each sentence beneath each index sentence. It will be good review.**

"Pray, then, in this way:
'Our Father who is in heaven, Hallowed be Your name.

_____

Your kingdom come.

_____

Your will be done, On earth as it is in heaven.

_____

Give us this day our daily bread.

_____

And forgive us our debts, as we also have forgiven our debtors.

_____

And do not lead us into temptation, but deliver us from evil.

_____

For Yours is the kingdom and the power and the glory forever. Amen' " (Matt. 6:9-13).

What singular personal pronouns did you circle or color?

List the plural personal pronouns you circled or colored.

What does this tell you about intercession?

The "us," "our," and "we" all let us know that prayer is not just about me. It includes others. When you pray "this way," the way Jesus taught us to pray, you are praying for yourself as well as for the body of Jesus Christ and the lost who have yet to hear and respond to the Great Shepherd (see John 10).

Therefore, each index sentence is meant to stimulate not only petition for yourself but also intercession for the body of Jesus Christ. We can appear before the throne of God on behalf of others. What a calling! What a ministry!

Even as I write this I have asked my husband, one of my sons, and my daughter-in-love (law), our staff, and our leaders to pray for me and this work God has called me to do. I feel so unworthy and inadequate as I realize I have so much to learn about the practice of prayer.

One of the delights of archaeologists is uncovering ancient mosaics, the handy work of artisans of the past. That's what I want us to do today, beloved— only the mosaic of intercession that we will uncover together will be one of exquisite design laid out by the master of artisans, God Himself. And wonder of wonders, you will find yourself there, right in His mosaic!

The first precious stone of truth is uncovered when we discover that the word "prayed" in Genesis 20:17 can also be translated *intercede*. It is the Hebrew word *palal*, which means "to intervene, interpose, pray." At least a dozen Hebrew words exist for *pray* and *prayer*. However, the most common word for *prayer* clearly is *tᵉpillâ* and the related verb, *palal*. Both the verb and the noun most frequently refer to intercessory prayer.

The first appearance of this word in Genesis 20:1-17 is in the context of one man, Abraham, interceding before God on behalf of Abimelech, a man who unknowingly took Abraham's wife, Sarah, to his tent, not realizing she was Abraham's wife. The result of Abraham's intercession was healing for Abimelech and Abimelech's wife whom God had struck with barrenness.

Read the story sometime as there is much more to it, but for now I simply want you to see that the components connected with the first use of *plal* are sin, intercession, and healing. Healing because of the intercession!

The second precious stone is in Exodus, where God instructed Aaron and his sons as to what they were to wear when they appeared in God's presence.

Read Exodus 28:1-6,9-12,15-22,29-30 in your Bible. As you read, look at these drawings from the *New Inductive Study Bible* so you have a visual aid of what is being described.

Ephod (viewed from the back)

Breastplate

**Draw a red heart over every reference to heart. I do this in my Bible because the heart is so important to God and is so often referred to. I don't want to miss what God wants me to know.
Stop and think about the why of it all. What is the picture God gave to the priests and the people? Can you see any parallel to intercession? Where?**

_____

_____

_____

Did you know that Isaiah 53 is one the clearest Old Testament prophecies about the Messiah, the Christ? Look at what Isaiah told us prophetically about Jesus in Isaiah 53:12. Note what He did and for whom He intercedes. Write it out, of course.

_____

_____

_____

_____

Let's uncover more. Read Isaiah 59:15-16. Note the situation and then what astonishes the Lord.

_____

_____

Did the situation sound similar to today? To our culture? What was needed?

_____

_____

What did He bring and how?

_____

_____

Let's move to the New Testament and behold the beauty of our Father's mosaic of intercession. The New Testament word for *intercession* is *huperentugchán*. It is quite a word, isn't it? It comes from two words: from *hupér* which means "for or on behalf of" and *entugchán*, which means "to turn to, appeal, to intercede for or in the behalf of someone, to plead for someone."

Look at what God tells us about Jesus Christ. Read Hebrews 4:14 and write what this verse tells you about Him.

_____

_____

As priests served under the Law, the Old Covenant, so we have a great high priest under the New Covenant—our Lord Jesus Christ. He is the priest who can sympathize with our weaknesses yet who is without sin (see Heb. 2:14-18; 4:15), One who has appeared in the presence of God for us (9:24). Hallelujah!

What is His ministry? Write Hebrews 7:25 below. It's beautiful.

_____

_____

_____

Are you asking, "Is this where I fit in?" Yes, beloved, because Jesus continuously intercedes for you before the Father. But there is even more!

Read Revelation 1:5-6 in your Bible. What do you see in these verses that places you in this beautiful mosaic of intercession?

_____

_____

_____

Now add Revelation 5:9-10 to your reading on intercession. From where did those who have been made a kingdom and priests to our God come?

_____

_____

_____

How do you think they came to this status? Do you think it had to do with the intercessory prayers of another child of God, another priest of God who took their calling seriously and interceded for your salvation? Who, and I am speaking figuratively now, interceded for you when you, like Abimelech, needed healing?

Beloved, do you see your high calling? Your ministry is to intercede in prayer for others who, though they are in a variety of situations, all need the touch of God in their lives. We'll see this as we continue looking at what Jesus taught about prayer.

As I share all this do you want to say, "But, Kay, sometimes I feel so inadequate, so filled with my weaknesses that I don't know how to pray. Sometimes all I can do is groan"? Could the groaning be the Spirit of God within you?

Read Romans 8:26-27. Put a cloud around every reference to the Spirit and underline every reference to "our," "we," and "us." Put a triangle over every reference to God. Watch the pronouns carefully, and match them with the right noun.

26 _"In the same way the Spirit also helps our weakness; for we do not know how to pray as we should, but the Spirit Himself intercedes for us with groanings too deep for words;_

27 _and He who searches the hearts knows what the mind of the Spirit is, because He intercedes for the saints according to the will of God."_

Faithful one, list what you learn about each one whom you marked. Let me get you started.

Us	The Spirit	God
1. we are weak	1. helps our weakness	1.

Awesome, isn't it! Jesus Christ intercedes from heaven for you. The Holy Spirit intercedes in you. You in turn, as a priest unto God, have the privilege of praying for and interceding for others—the lost and the saved.

You can do kingdom work all around the world on your knees in your closet alone or gathered with the congregation of fellow believers, members of the church, the body of Jesus Christ of which He is the head.

Can you really comprehend all that God does with your prayers, precious one? Do you realize how important they are to Him? To His kingdom?

IT'S TIME TO PRAY

Why don't you sit quietly before the Lord and ask Him to lay a specific person on your heart and mind. Ask God how to pray for this person, to lead you in prayer on her behalf.

If you don't know where to begin, try "walking" her through prayer by using the pattern of the Lord's Prayer. Begin by either thanking God for _____'s salvation or by praying for it so _____ can truly pray, "Our Father."

Next pray that she would hallow His name, give Him her total allegiance, and so forth. Have a blessed time interceding, dear one.

DAY 3 | **A Faith That Soars**

"Give us this day our daily bread." Before we look at this fourth index sentence which deals with petition, asking God to provide, let me ask you a question. Have you ever been embarrassed or even afraid to pray for specific things for fear God wouldn't answer your prayer? I have.

I have thought, *Father, what if You don't answer this prayer? It's going to look as if prayer doesn't work!* At this point some of you may be laughing at me. I don't blame you, because I'm laughing too! I can hear you saying, "Kay, why put the blame on God if the prayer is not answered? Why not put it on yourself?"

I'll tell you why! I felt I was claiming faith in His character and His ways. If God didn't come through, it would look as if He had failed—not me! Let me give you an illustration from when I was about three or four years old in the Lord. (I have come to trust my Father more and to relax in His ways.)

Jack and I were missionaries in Mexico and had taken a group of English-speaking teens on a weekend retreat. Conditions were primitive, but the girls had the best end of the deal. We had an army surplus tent over our heads.

That night as we sat around the campfire and I taught, God really spoke. Several missionary kids who thought they were saved came to the Lord that evening. I am wary of emotional decisions around campfires, so I did not offer an invitation. Even so, from out of the dark they came, separately, many in tears, telling me they had turned to God and were willing to follow Him totally. God had moved! Time proved the reality of those commitments.

Well, you can imagine the joy in the tent that night. You know how girls are! They were at fever pitch when all of a sudden we heard a loud, agonized, "Oh, no! I've dropped my contact lens! My parents will kill me."

Now, you know missionary parents are not allowed to kill their children; it's a bad testimony! Because Gail was rather wild and had been kicked out of several Christian schools, she may have been right—it might have crossed their minds. Contacts weren't disposable in those days, and they were expensive. This was a brand-new one she had gotten to replace another one she had just lost! Replacing contacts is hard on missionary support funds!

At any rate, we were all down on our knees with lanterns held above our heads as we looked in green grass for a green-tinted contact! As I crawled in the grass, God reminded me that I had just been teaching these teens about His attributes and His ways. *Ask Me to find it,* came the thought. *Ask Me in front of the girls.*

A silent debate ensued. *But, Father, what if I ask You and we don't find it? How is that going to look?* I went back to my groping, but I couldn't help thinking, *He does know where it is because He is omniscient, all-knowing. There is not a thing hidden from His sight.* Still I resisted; it was too risky. We might not find it. Then how would God look? I had better not risk His reputation in front of ones so young in the faith. (Can you understand what I was going through?)

Well, God won. I called the search to a temporary halt and there on my knees prayed aloud. As I did, I reminded God fervently of every promise I could think of that related to our plight. It was not a short prayer as my faith really needed biblical fuel!

After I finished, we continued to search for a while to the intermittent tune of Gail's swan song, one short chorus, "My parents are gonna kill me! My parents are gonna kill me!"

When I was almost ready to tell God I never should have prayed aloud, Lily let out a hysterical yelp, "I found it! I found it!" Tears poured down her face. But why? These weren't gushy, sentimental, girlish tears.

I didn't have to wait long to find out. Of all the teens, none was more exemplary in behavior or zeal for missions than Lily. Any one of us would have willingly claimed her as our own. She would have made us look like ideal missionary parents! Lily claimed to have been saved at a very young age, and her behavior gave us no cause to doubt the reality of her profession. She was the opposite of dear Gail! Yet here was that precious girl, tears streaming down her face, half laughing and half crying as she told us her story.

After the lesson around the campfire, Lily realized she really had never been saved. It was hard for her to believe, since she had led so many others to Christ. Yet she knew it was true, so there in the dark the transaction had taken place. Lily passed from death to life, from the power of Satan to the kingdom of God. She received forgiveness of sins and inheritance among those who are sanctified (Acts 26:18). She had been coming into the tent to tell us when Gail went into hysterics over her contact.

While I was on my knees looking for the contact and wrestling with God about praying aloud, Lily was praying: "God, You have never directly answered my prayers all these years. Now that I am Yours, prove it by answering this prayer. Let me find Gail's contact."

Oh, what a precious Father we have! God orchestrated it all by His Spirit because it delighted His Father's heart to confirm her salvation in an answer to very specific prayer.

"Give us this day our daily bread" is a very specific request and a specific prayer that demonstrates our faith. In the light of that experience and in preparation for our study of what it means to ask for daily bread, let me share some truths about faith that I believe will be helpful. We touched on faith at the beginning of our study, but now it is time to go deeper because we have come to the issue of specific prayer. Hebrews 11 is called the "Faith Chapter." If you were to color every occurrence of faith in its 40 verses, you would readily understand why.

Read Hebrews 11:1-3 in your Bible. Then copy Hebrews 11:1 below. As you write it, I want you to do it in a structured way. Also as you write it, say it aloud. You need to hear the words.

Now _____ __ __ _____ __ _____ _____ for,

the _____ __ _____ ____ seen.

Read Hebrews 11:2. In one word, how did men gain approval?

_____

According to verse 3, how were the worlds prepared? How do you know? Were you there?

_____

_____

How does anyone know the truth of Hebrews 11:3?

_____

_____

Over and over again you will find God reminding His people that He is the Creator of the heavens and the earth. It is one of the fundamentals of a biblical worldview and a matter you need to settle that is determined only by faith. Either you believe God or you believe a theory of man, some claim of science. Whom will you believe?

Believe me, your faith will never truly soar until you believe God.

What is faith? The Greek word for faith is *pistis*. A firm persuasion, a conviction based upon hearing. *Pistis* is kinfolk with the Greek word *peitho*, persuade. Faith is simply taking God at His Word. It's believing that the Bible is the Word of God.

True faith, not head knowledge, is a firm conviction that brings personal surrender to God and His Word. In turn, our personal surrender is manifested in our conduct, in the way we live. James made it clear that our works demonstrate the reality of our faith. True faith has evidence. The same thing is clearly stated in 1 John. You could easily see it if you were to mark every reference to "know" and then look at what God says you know and how you know it. This is not an assignment, just a suggestion for the future. I mentioned it earlier in our study, but we have covered so much that it bears repeating.

If God by His word prepared and created the world, can He not by His same powerful Word take care of what He created? Of course. We need to say with Jeremiah the prophet, "Ah! Lord God! Behold, You have made the heavens and the earth by Your great power and by Your outstretched arm! Nothing is too difficult for You" (Jer. 32:17) and then hear God respond, "Behold, I am the LORD, the God of all flesh; is anything too difficult for Me?" (v. 27).

In telling us to pray for our daily bread—or tomorrow's bread as some interpret it—Jesus was reminding us that our lives are to be lived in total dependence on God day-by-day. And faith says, Amen! He is able!

In Matthew 6:25-34 Jesus, in a sense, expanded on this life of total dependence by telling us we are not to worry saying, "'What will we eat?' or 'What will we drink?' or 'What will we wear for clothing?' For the Gentiles eagerly seek all these things; for your heavenly Father knows that you need all these things." He knows, beloved. He knows, and He is able to supply all your needs according to His riches in Christ Jesus our Lord (Phil. 4:19). You are an heir of God, a joint heir with Jesus Christ. You belong to God.

Pause and think that through: *You* belong to God. "Ask, and it will be given to you … If you then, being evil, know how to give good gifts to your children, how much more will your Father who is in heaven give what is good to those who ask Him!" (Matt. 7:7,11).

Is your heart burning with desire for God—for pleasing Him with your faith? Mine is. I think, *Oh Father, Father, I long to live this way. I long to remember. Remind me, remind me. It is so very simple. You say it and I am to believe it. And when I do, I bring You pleasure. Oh God, I want to bring You pleasure.*

IT'S TIME TO PRAY

Is it really time to pray? I'm not so sure. I think it is time to be still, to sit in Your presence, Father, and to think about living for Your pleasure. Living by faith. For without faith it is impossible to please You.

I must believe You are God, a rewarder of those who seek You; and I must live accordingly. Selah.

DAY 4 | **Total Dependence on God**

Prayer is a demonstration of your total dependence on God. Thus a major precept of prayer is asking. You may not like that. You may think you ought to be woman enough to get what you need on your own. But, precious one, if this is what you think, let me gently tell you that you are wrong. To try and have your needs of the soul, body, spirit, or mind met apart from seeking Him is to miss some of the riches of His glory that could be yours.

Read James 4:1-3 in your Bible. Circle every occurrence of "you" and mark "ask" in the same way have been marking "prayer." Then answer these questions.

• What's the conflict? How is it described?

_____

• Why does the conflict exist?

_____

_____

• Why are they asking and not receiving?

_____

_____

• Do you know anyone like this? What is that person's life like?

_____

_____

Now read James 4:4. What's the problem?

_____

_____

_____

To try and have your needs met
- apart from seeking God will end in internal war. Riddled with lust and envy, the desire to satisfy *your* pleasures causes "war" within (Jas. 4:1-3).
- apart from trusting in God will end in quarrels and conflicts (v. 1).
- independently of God is to deny your need of Him (Phil. 4:19).

To go to others for help instead of to your Father is to live a life of woe. "Woe to those who go down to Egypt [where you once were in bondage] for help and rely on horses, and trust in chariots because they are many and in horsemen because they are very strong, but they do not look to the Holy One of Israel, nor seek the LORD!" (Isa. 31:1).

To rely on yourself is to live in a stony wilderness. "Thus says the LORD, 'Cursed is the man who trusts in mankind and makes flesh his strength, and whose heart turns away from the LORD. For he will be like a bush in the desert and will not see when prosperity comes, but will live in stony wastes in the wilderness, a land of salt without inhabitant'" (Jer. 17:5-6).

But to live in total dependence on God is to be blessed. "Blessed is the man who trusts in the LORD and whose trust is the LORD. For he will be like a tree planted by the water, that extends its roots by a stream and will not fear when the heat comes; but its leaves will be green, and it will not be anxious in a year of drought nor cease to yield fruit" (Jer. 17:7-8).

Why, oh, why will we not humble ourselves, get rid of our pride, and realize that apart from God we can do nothing, not even supply our own needs?

"But," you may say, "those who do not know Jesus supply their own needs and they survive!" Yes, they do survive. But how? Where's their peace, confidence, pleasure, and assurance? If it is not in God, where is it? And if it is not in God, what will they do when the source is taken away? God is *El Olam*, the everlasting God. He can never be taken away. He will never go away. He is always there—omnipresent day after day; and He's only a prayer, a cry, away.

> *"This I know, that God is for me. In God whose word I praise,*
> *   In the LORD, whose word I praise,*
> *In God I have put my trust, I shall not be afraid.*
> *   What can man do to me?"* (Ps. 56:9-11).

One of my favorite little books is *On This Day* by Robert J. Morgan. It's a book of 365 amazing and inspiring stories about saints, martyrs, and heroes. I want to share "God's Handwriting," with you, because it will encourage and delight you with the practicality of depending on God. You'll love Morgan's books.

Missionaries Dick and Margaret Hillis found themselves caught in China during the Japanese invasion. The couple lived with their two children in the inland town of Shenkiu. The village was tense with fear; every day brought terrifying reports of the Japanese advance. At the worst possible time, Dick developed appendicitis, and he knew his life depended on making the long journey by ricksha to the hospital. On January 15, 1941, with deep foreboding, Margaret watched him leave.

Soon the Chinese colonel came with news. The enemy was near and townspeople must evacuate. Margaret shivered, knowing that one-year-old Johnny and two-month-old Margaret Anne would never survive as refugees. So she stayed put. Early next morning she tore the page from the wall calendar and read the new day's Scripture. It was Psalm 56:3—*What time I am afraid, I will trust in thee.*

The town emptied during the day, and next morning Margaret arose, feeling abandoned. The new verse on the calendar was Psalm 9:10—*Thou, Lord, hast not forsaken them that seek thee.*

The next morning she arose to distant sounds of gunfire and worried about food for her children. The calendar verse was Genesis 50:21—*I will nourish you and your little ones.* An old woman suddenly popped in with a pail of steaming goat's milk, and another straggler arrived with a basket of eggs.

Through the day, sounds of warfare grew louder, and during the night Margaret prayed for deliverance. The next morning she tore the page from the calendar to read Psalm 56:9—*When I cry unto Thee, then shall my enemies turn back.* The battle was looming closer, and Margaret didn't go to bed that night. Invasion seemed imminent. But the next morning, all was quiet. Suddenly, villagers began returning to their homes, and the colonel knocked on her door.

For some reason, he told her, the Japanese had withdrawn their troops. No one could understand it, but the danger had passed. They were safe.

Margaret glanced at her wall calendar and felt she had been reading the handwriting of God.[3]

You and I have the handwriting of God—the words of God—and it is He who tells us to ask for our daily bread, who tells us not to worry about tomorrow, for tomorrow will care of itself. Each day has troubles of its own.

According to Matthew 6:33, what is your task?

_____

_____

What is His promise (v. 33)?

_____

_____

(If you don't know or remember what "these things" are, read
 Matt. 6:25-33.)
        Print Matthew 6:31-34 on several index cards and put
them in strategic places. Every time you see the cards, read the
passage aloud until you've memorized it.

We are to do our job and let God do His! We will always mess up when we try
to take over for God. Plus, He'll never tolerate it. Remember we cannot please
Him if we refuse to believe Him. We settled that when we read Hebrews 11:6.

IT'S TIME TO PRAY

It's time to ask God to search your heart, precious one, and see
if there's any hurtful way, any way of pain in you because you
are not walking in total dependence on Him. Ask Him to show
you any way, place, area, or arena in which you are trying to do
His job. Write down any insights God gives you and then calling
them exactly what they are, ask Him to forgive you. He promises
He will cleanse you from all unrighteousness (1 John 1:9).

_____

_____

_____

DAY 5 | **The Lord Who Provides**

Today's study has more pages, but don't let them scare you. I've included two
stories that will bless your soul.

        From praying for such magnanimous matters as God's kingdom coming
to earth to asking for daily bread, forgiveness of sins and deliverance from evil
and the Evil One—this, dear child of God, is the scope of what it means to cry
in prayer "Abba, Father."

        Praying God's way means to live in total dependence on our Father, pray-
ing without ceasing. Why? Because in Him we live and move and have our
being. Worshiping, giving allegiance, submitting to His will, asking for our
needs to be met, confessing our sins, and seeking His protection is the way to

pray for ourselves and for others who now belong to the family or who will belong to the forever family of God!

What I said earlier bears repeating: asking in prayer pleases God for it demonstrates our total dependence on Him as our Father. How then do we ask? In our final day of study this week I want to make sure you and I understand the 1,2,3,4, and 5 of it.

First, we are to ask. We are neither to assume nor take for granted that whatever we need will come. Every time we ask it shows that we acknowledge God as the source of all things. This is why, I believe, Jesus says, "Give us this day our daily bread." It is to be a day-by-day dependence.

A contemporary teaching that grieves my heart is prosperity teaching. We often hear about the answers to prayers for prosperity but not the damage to the faith of listeners who hear name-it-and-claim-it teaching telling them we are "King's kids" and our Father God wants us to have the very best and a lot of it. Jesus' instruction to ask for "daily bread" contradicts that teaching!

In our society it is difficult to understand "daily bread," but such concepts were not difficult to understand in biblical times or even now in many other places in the world. One morning as I showered and dressed, I was listening to Deuteronomy on my CD player. In that time a laborer was to be paid his daily wage before the sun set because it was his daily sustenance. Immediately, Jesus' instruction on prayer came to mind.

One of my favorite illustrations goes back to the days of Communism in Romania before the death of Nicolae Ceausescu in 1989. When I finished reading the story, all I could do was weep and worship my God.

> Christmas was not to be the same this year. Isolated from the rest of the outside world, it was difficult with the seven children to celebrate the birth of Jesus when their stomachs were empty. There were no decorations, no brightly lit candles, no Christmas tree, no cookies, and no beautifully wrapped gifts to exchange. The children were just as hungry today as any other day. Soon, Dad would be telling the children about the Messiah, born in a manger, much like the little hut they lived in.
>
> This father, mother, and their seven children (all under 14) were banished into exile in the far reaches of an uninhabited part of the country. The Communist authorities hated the father because of his convicting preaching. He was nicknamed by the believers, "The Golden Word," because of his eloquence. They were forced to move to a little village, inaccessible by car or train. What little food they were given was flown in by helicopter. They lived in a tiny hut with a straw roof, under constant surveillance of the prison guards.
>
> The village was established for those "undesirables" of society, which includes "religious fanatics." The stinging chill was made worse by the wind whipping snow across the flat barren land, unbroken by hills, and whistling its song through every crack and crevice

in the small hut. For two days now the guards had not bothered to bring them any food. They were too busy preparing their own celebration with wine and pork. The children listened intently to their father telling them the story of Jesus, huddled together around the dim light of the gas lantern on the table. They were so intent, they forgot about their hunger. But when the story was over, one after the other began to cry. Before going to bed that Christmas Eve, the whole family knelt down on the dirt floor and prayed as never before: "Our Father, which are in Heaven … Give us this day our daily bread."

After they finished their prayer and said, "Amen," the children asked their mother and father many questions.

"Do you think God heard our prayer?"

"Of course He did."

"But what if He didn't hear it?"

"That isn't possible," the father replied.

"Do you think He will send us bread?" they asked.

"Yes, I'm sure He will," said the father.

"But when?" they cried.

The parents, heartbroken to see their children crying from hunger, could not answer. The children continued. "Who will He send to bring us bread?"

"He will find someone," said the father reassuringly.

"But what if He doesn't find anyone?"

"Well then," the father paused, "He Himself will bring it with His own hand. Now close your eyes and go to sleep."

The father blew out the little lantern as darkness descended on them, and the wind whistled to them in their sleep. Suddenly, the still darkness was shattered by a knock on the door!

The father got out of bed and opened the door just a crack to keep the cold from blowing inside. A hand holding a large loaf of bread was stretched toward him. His heart pounding, the father reached out to take the bread, and at the same time opened the door widely to say thank you. But at that very moment, in the twinkling of an eye, the hand was gone, and there was no one there. Bewildered, the father closed the door and turned around. All seven children leaped out of bed and surrounded him.

"Who was it, Dad? Who gave you the bread?"

"Children," he said with a tremble in his voice, "The Lord did not find anyone to send to us with bread, so He Himself came and gave it to us with His own hand."

Nobody could sleep. … The children couldn't stop singing about how the Lord had spread a table for them in the wilderness.

Second, know you and I are to ask within the boundaries of God's Word. When it comes to asking for anything, I personally believe daily bread is whatever I need to sustain me through a day. The Word of God reveals the will of God.

> Mark each reference to prayer and record what the verse/passage teaches you about prayer. Or write out what the verse says. Reading it aloud helps too.

Psalm 145:17-19

_____

_____

_____

_____

The Whole Counsel of God

By the way, weigh everything you hear and read about prayer against the whole counsel of God. When Paul was about to depart for Jerusalem, he gathered the elders from Ephesus and reminded them that he had shared the whole counsel of God with them and that they were to beware because, after his departure, grievous wolves would come in and seek to lead people astray (Acts 20:25-32).

If anyone suggests you lay aside the Bible when it comes to prayer, a red flag of danger ought to go up immediately. Remember the Spirit of God never works apart from or contrary to the Word of God.

John 14:13-14

_____

_____

_____

John 15:7

_____

_____

_____

John 15:16

_____

_____

I can't resist sharing two more verses from Ephesians (3:20-21). I love these verses and often use them in prayer. As you read them aloud, mark the word *ask* as you have marked *prayer*.

> 20 *"Now to Him who is able to do far more abundantly beyond all that we ask or think, according to the power that works within us,*
> 21 *to Him be the glory in the church and in Christ Jesus to all generations forever and ever. Amen."*

When you pray, learn to plead the promises of God. "For as many as are the promises of God, in Him they are yes" (2 Cor. 1:20). D. L. Moody, the great evangelist used so mightily by God in America and England in the late 1800s, said, "Tarry at a promise and God will meet you there."

Because the Bible is my prayer book, I have prayed Scripture for years; yet this wonderful principle of pleading the promises of God was crystallized for me years ago when I read this from Armin Gesswein's *School of Prayer.*

> Early in the ministry I had an experience that completely changed my understanding of prayer. What a transformation! I was called to start churches and had just discovered "prayer meeting truth" in the Acts. So I started a prayer meeting—the first one I ever attended.
>
> In came an elderly Methodist one night. When he prayed, I detected something new. "I have never heard praying like that," I said to myself. It was not only fervency—I had plenty of that. Heaven and earth got together at once when he prayed. There was a strange immediacy about it. The prayer and the answer were not far apart—in fact they were moving along together. He had it "in the bag" so it seemed to me. The Holy Spirit was right there, in action, giving him assurance of the answer even while he was praying! When I prayed, God was "way out there," somewhere in the distance, listening. The answer, too, was in the distance, in the by and by.
>
> Eager to learn his secret, I went to see him one day. His name was Ambrose Whaley, and everyone called him "Uncle Am." He was a retired blacksmith—also a Methodist lay preacher. I soon came to the point, "Uncle Am, I would love to pray with you." At once he arose, led me outside across the driveway into a red barn, up a ladder, into a haymow! There, in some old hay, lay two big Bibles—one open. "What is this?" I thought. I prayed first, as I recall it. Poured out my heart, needs, burdens, wishes, aspirations, ambitions to God. Then he prayed—and there was "that difference" again. There, in that hay, on our knees, at the eyeball level, I said: "Uncle Am, what is it? ... you have some kind of a secret in praying. Would you mind sharing it with me?"

I was 24, he was 73 (he lived to be 93), and with an eagle-look in his eyes, he said: "YOUNG MAN, LEARN TO PLEAD THE PROMISES OF GOD!"

That did it! My praying has never been the same since. That word completely changed my understanding of prayer. It really revolutionized it! I "saw it" as soon as he said it. Saw what? Well—when I prayed there was fervency, ambition, etc. (The Lord does not put a "perfect squelch" on these either.) But I lacked FAITH. Prayer is the key to heaven, but faith unlocks the door. THERE MUST BE FAITH. Where does that come from? From hearing … the WORD OF GOD. Uncle Am would plead Scripture after Scripture, reminding Him of promise after promise, pleading these like a lawyer does his case—the Holy Spirit pouring in His assurance of being heard. This man knew the promises "by the bushel." … I soon learned that he was a mighty intercessor. … He prayed THROUGH THE BIBLE. He taught me the secret of intercessory praying. How can I ever thank God enough for leading me to such a prayer warrior!

WHAT HAPPENED? With this discovery, God really GAVE ME A NEW BIBLE! I had not yet learned how to make the Bible MY PRAYER BOOK. It gave me a new motivation for Bible study. I began to "dig in"! I would now search the Scriptures … meditate … mark its many promises … memorize, memorize, MEMORIZE! There are thousands of promises: a promise for every need, burden, problem, situation.

"YOUNG MAN, LEARN TO PLEAD THE PROMISES OF GOD!"[4]

Uncle Am wasn't the only one who pled the promises of God! He had a long line of predecessors. Search the Old Testament, observe the prayers of men and women of God, and you will find them constantly reminding God of His promises to Abraham, Isaac, and Jacob, to His covenant people Israel.

Third, you must ask according to the will of God. Why do I separate on this third point the Word of God from the will of God when it is the Word that reveals His will? I do it because you must wait on God in prayer to find out if something is His specific will for you and when it would be His will for it to happen! So often we hear of how God answered others' prayers, and we expect the same thing.

It's not always the same because God has a specific work for each of us to do. We saw that in Ephesians 2:10, and it comes out also in Jesus' response to Peter in John 21:20-22. This is also supported in Hebrews 11:32-38.

Some believers had glorious deliveries. Others suffered greatly. But God was with them all. They lived by faith, taking God at His Word. When you ask, remember you've said to God, "Your will be done, on earth as it is in heaven."

Fourth, you are to ask until the answer comes. Asking is not a one-time event. You must never despair of persevering; it keeps you in His presence, where you'll experience fullness of joy and pleasures evermore.

Take a moment and read Luke 18:1-8 in your Bible, remembering parables are told for a reason.

• What did Jesus say is the purpose of this parable (v. 1)?

_____

_____

• Mark the references to prayer. Don't miss the words used to describe persevering prayer in verse 7. Also mark "heart," and you will see how it relates to persistent prayer. Now what do you learn for yourself in regard to prayer?

_____

_____

_____

When scholars traced the source of the Scottish revival, they found two praying women. These women prayed so long and so diligently without seeing anything happen that one of them in her weariness cried out, "God, if you don't send revival, then I'm not going to speak to You again!"

Fifth and finally, remember when you ask, ask for others. Jesus' instructions were "give us *our* daily bread" (italics added). Every church, every ministry, each believer needs those who will take our needs before the throne of Jehovah-Jireh, the Lord who provides.

IT'S TIME TO PRAY

What is it, beloved, that you need? If you don't have any needs, what is it others (a friend, your church, or a ministry) need? Review the need in light of the five points we looked at today, and then pray accordingly.

1. Basil Miller, *George Muller: Man of Faith and Miracles* (Minneapolis: Bethany House Publishers, 1941), 50-51.
2. Ibid.
3. Robert J. Morgan, *On This Day* (Nashville: Thomas Nelson Publishers, 1997), January 15.
4. Armin Gesswin, "Plead the Promises of God!" in *School of Prayer* (Pasadena, CA: International Intercessors).

WEEKENDER

Learning to pray God's way according to His Word becomes a pattern when we spend time with Him every day. Each week this Weekender page helps you include time with Him in your weekend schedule. As you refresh from the week, don't miss a day in the Word and in communication with the Father.

How is your prayer life demonstrating your commitment to depend totally on God?

_____

_____

_____

_____

_____

How has God been answering your prayers this week?

_____

_____

_____

_____

_____

YOU BELONG TO GOD

SESSION 4 • YOU BELONG TO GOD

Index Sentence 4: "Give us this day our daily bread."

We move from our focus on God to a focus on our own _____ _____.

We forget that He is:

Jehovah-Jireh (our provider)

Jehovah-Shammah (one who is there)

Jehovah-Tsidkenu (our Righteousness)

Jehovah-Shalom (peace)

_____ is idolatry.

His message to us is this: _____ _____ _____. Instead we are in an attitude of praying without ceasing.

Intercession on behalf of our personal needs

Stories about God's Provision: What stories are you able to tell?

You're not worried because you know _____ _____ _____.

What are you and I to do?

"Seek first His kingdom and His righteousness, and all these things will be added to you" (Matt. 6:33).

"Give us (not just me) our daily bread."

It's awesome to experience _____ _____.

It's awesome to be _____ _____ _____.

NOTES

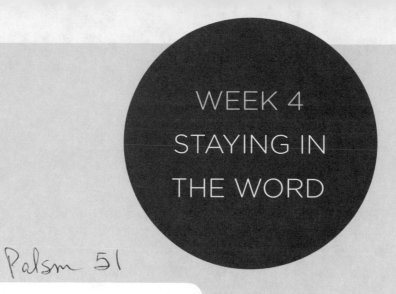

WEEK 4
STAYING IN
THE WORD

Palsm 51

Goals for the week

- RECOGNIZE and act on my need to confess sin

- COMMIT to forgive others just as God forgives me

- INTERCEDE for God's people

- GUARD against temptation

- CONTINUE to pray the Lord's Prayer as a powerful pattern for today

Don't you just love your relationship with the Father, beloved? I was reminded again this week how powerful prayer can be when it starts and ends with worshiping God. I will miss our time together. But I know that if you continue to discipline yourself to discover truth for yourself and live in the light of it, God will bring you to even greater maturity and usefulness in His kingdom.

Pray, precious one, pray.

DAY 1: When Our Prayers Seem to Hit the Ceiling

DAY 2: Forgiveness Is Our Response to God

DAY 3: The Heart of an Intercessor

DAY 4: Guard Duty for the Body

DAY 5: Our Hallelujah of Worship

DAY 1 | When Our Prayers Seem to Hit the Ceiling

Can a child of God ignore the will of God for his or her life, walk in rebellion, and continue to have His blessing of answered prayer? No, beloved, that is not possible. Jesus told us that we are to ask for God's forgiveness when we don't live righteously before Him. Before we look at the Scriptures and see what God says on this critical issue, let me share a story about what happened to one of our leaders when she heard the truths you are about to study. She relates:

> Our home had not sold in more than two years of being on the market. Every time someone came close to purchasing it, the deal fell through. A lady rented it, devastated it, stopped paying rent, and moved out, leaving the house in total disarray.
>
> I thought, *Lord I know I am Your child, but I don't know why I feel as if my prayers are hitting the ceiling.* We had lost over $11,000 on the home and still hadn't sold it. Each month was an increase of loss in our savings. So I bought the book *Lord, Teach Me to Pray in 28 Days* to discover what could be going on with my prayers not being heard.
>
> Soon I discovered through the study that my 14-year addiction (I was 28 years old) to smoking cigarettes was coming between the Lord and me. I smoked just a few cigarettes a day and had ignored the Holy Spirit's convictions in the past. But now I heard the Lord speak to my heart very clearly about how those nasty cigarettes were coming before Him because I had continued to ignore His desire for me not to smoke. I cried hard that evening, mourning the fact of what I was doing.
>
> I cried also because I knew I had tried several times before to quit, but could not come clean of the addiction. Every time I passed the back porch the habit would call me, especially in the evening. I was afraid that I would heed the call. So that night I prayed. I recognized my sin, acknowledging the fact that I could not quit on my own, but that I wanted to—very badly. I did not want anything to come between the Lord and me in our relationship and my prayers to Him.
>
> But the Lord would have to deliver me, so I asked that He help me overcome and be free of the habit. Needless to say, He healed me of this addiction. I have not desired to smoke since that evening, which is amazing to me!
>
> The experience made me realize that God truly is my healer. Within a month of this experience, our house sold. Within the year, my husband and I received a check for $14,000 which recovered our losses. God is a good God.

I believe God did this for me to be healed, to learn of Him, to teach me how to pray and how to approach Him when I come to Him in prayer—without rebellion in my life. When we are in the midst of rebellion, we can't casually approach God in prayer thinking He will ignore our sin and bless us anyway.

Now let's consider the fifth index sentence in the Lord's Prayer. It is critical to our relationship with God because the kingdom of God is all about dealing with sin and finding forgiveness. Read it carefully: "Forgive us our debts, as we also have forgiven our debtors." You might want to underline "as we also" and think about what Jesus was teaching in respect to how we are to pray.

As you look at these index sentences, you realize there must be a purpose in their order. Nothing God does is ever random. That is why I wondered, *Father, why are sin and forgiveness not dealt with immediately?*

As I thought about this question, it seemed that if I were to confess sin and to seek to forgive my brother before I did anything else in prayer, the cleansing might be superficial and would probably make forgiveness of others even more difficult. Why? Because the immediate focus in prayer would be on myself. However, when I begin prayer in worship, long for His kingdom, commit myself to the will of God even as it is done in heaven, and come to my Father seeking His provision for my needs—then confession of the debt of righteousness that I owe Him cannot help but follow!

Let's reason together: How can you and I genuinely worship God, tell Him we desire His will, ask Him to supply our needs, and not be overwhelmed with our sin, with our need of His favor in forgiveness? Having come to this point and knowing His forgiveness, how can we withhold forgiveness from those who have trespassed against us, especially when their transgressions against us, fellow sinners, are so miniscule in comparison to our transgressions against the holiness of God?

Think about it, beloved. Stop for a minute and reflect on what you just read. If you read it quickly, maybe you need to read it again. I want you to follow the logic of the order Jesus gave us in prayer.

God cannot overlook sin. The very nature of His being forbids it. God is holy; He is absolutely righteous and pure. He is totally, absolutely separate from humanity and thus separate and separated from sin. And because God is holy, sin must always be dealt with. The history of Israel testifies to it.

If you studied nothing but the Torah—the first five books of the Bible— you know Israel is suffering today because they collectively do not honor God as God; they don't live by His commandments. They are a divided people seeking to serve God and man, and no one can serve two masters. Therefore, they are reaping the harvest of disobedience. God knew it would happen. He spelled out the consequences of disobedience (and their restoration) very clearly in Deuteronomy 27–30. Those consequences have and continue to come to pass. Yet rest assured, the Holy One of Israel is their redeemer (see Isa. 41:14). Israel will be chastened but not forsaken because the gifts and calling of God are irrevocable (see Rom. 11:29).

Israel is our visual aid, a constant reminder that sin must be dealt with. And it is the same for the true child of God. Hebrews 12, the "chastening or disciplining chapter," tells us whom the Lord loves He disciplines and He does it so that we might be partakers of His holiness (vv. 6,10).

> Read Hebrews 12:9-11 in your Bible and watch for the word "chastened" (KJV) or "discipline" (NASB). When you finish, write what God's discipline yields and who benefits. This last question, "who benefits" pertains to you and me, so don't miss it.
>
> • The fruit of discipline is _____ .
>
> • Those who benefit from God's discipline are those who
>
> _____ .
>
> • Has God ever disciplined you, dear one? How do you respond?
>
> _____

The word for discipline is *paideia*. It is the sum total of child training. Obviously, part of our child training is to pray "forgive us our debts, as we also have forgiven our debtors."

Now then, precious child of God, if you want to see the holiness of God, take a long, careful look at Calvary. Who crucified His only begotten Son on Golgotha's hill of shame? Who let Jesus scream, "MY GOD, MY GOD, WHY HAVE YOU FORSAKEN ME?" (Matt. 27:46)? Who let Jesus taste death for all (Heb. 2:9)?

It was the One with eyes too pure to behold iniquity (Ps. 22:1-3; Hab. 1:13). It was the One not satisfied with the blood of bulls and goats, which could never take away sin (Heb. 10:4-8). It was the One who said, "Without shedding of blood there is no forgiveness" (9:22). It was the One who at Calvary satisfied His holiness when the sinless Lamb of God was slaughtered by the Father ... the Lamb "who takes away the sin of the world" (John 1:29).

In His holiness He "[God] made Him [Jesus] who knew no sin to be sin on our behalf, so that we might become the righteousness of God in Him" (2 Cor. 5:21). "But," you may say, "if all my sins were forgiven at Calvary, why must I confess them again, asking His forgiveness? Are they not already forgiven?" Yes, all sin—past, present, and future—was dealt with at Calvary. "We have been sanctified through the offering of the body of Jesus Christ once for all" (Heb. 10:10).

Although sin was paid for in full at Calvary, sin unconfessed and unforsaken before the throne of God puts a barrier between God and His child.

Listen to the Word of the Lord and mark every reference to prayer and to sin (including synonyms such as *not listening to God's law, iniquity,* and *doing evil*). Put a big S over sin or color it brown. Mark *prayer* as you've been doing. Read each verse carefully. Listen to the heart of God as He speaks of sin.

> *He who turns away his ear from listening to the law, even his prayer is an abomination" (Prov. 28:9).*

> 1 *"Behold, the LORD's hand is not so short that it cannot save; nor is His ear so dull that it cannot hear.*
> 2 *But your iniquities have made a separation between you and your God, and your sins have hidden His face from you so that He does not hear" (Isa. 59:1-2).*

> *"If I regard wickedness in my heart, the Lord will not hear" (Ps. 66:18).*

> *"FOR THE EYES OF THE LORD ARE UPON THE RIGHTEOUS, AND HIS EARS ATTEND TO THEIR PRAYER, BUT THE FACE OF THE LORD IS AGAINST THOSE WHO DO EVIL" (1 Pet. 3:12).*

> *"Therefore, confess your sins to one another, and pray for one another so that you may be healed. The effective prayer of a righteous man can accomplish much" (Jas. 5:16).*

Reason with me. If there is no need to confess our sins because Jesus has paid for them, then why would Jesus include this as an integral part of prayer?

When Jesus said, "Forgive us our debts," He was talking about our moral debts, our sins. We owe God absolute righteousness. To sin is to be in debt! Every time we do not act righteously (do what God says is right), we are in debt to God and must ask forgiveness. We have offended our holy Father.

Write 1 John 1:9 below. As you record it, say the words aloud.

_____

_____

The word translated "confess" is *homologeo* and means "to say the same thing." In other words, you name sin for what it is; you call it what God calls sin.

It's time to name any sin that needs to be confessed and to ask God to forgive you the debt of righteousness you owe Him. I can tell you with the voice of experience that it is wonderful to know you are right with God.

IT'S TIME TO PRAY

Read King David's prayer of confession in Psalm 51. Ask God to reveal to you any debt of righteousness you owe Him. Then pay that debt by agreeing with God, confessing your sin.

You might want to take a piece of paper and write down everything God shows you. When you finish, write over it 1 John 1:9, tear up the piece of paper, and throw it away.

You have His Word. Proverbs 28:13 says, "He who conceals his transgressions will not prosper, but he who confesses and forsakes them will find compassion." Listen to your Father, "But to this one I will look, to him who is humble and contrite of spirit, and who trembles at My word" (Isa. 66:2).

DAY 2 | Forgiveness Is Our Response to God

Now then, beloved, are you ready for a touchy subject? Forgiving others. Book after book has been written on the subject; have you ever wondered why? Because it is difficult to forgive, especially if what has been done to you is cruel and sick. We can come up with 100 reasons or more not to forgive. Among them, "If I forgive them, they'll get away with the awful thing they did." Or we reason, "What they did to me was so destructive; they ruined my life. They don't deserve to be forgiven."

A myriad of reasons exists not to forgive, and many of them are quite logical, seemingly very reasonable. But His words still stand. We are to forgive, and the forgiveness we seek from God is in direct correlation to our willingness to forgive others: "forgive us our debts, as we also have forgiven our debtors."

No sooner did Jesus finish teaching them the way to pray than He returned immediately to the issue of forgiveness. It is as if He wanted to make certain we understood the necessity to forgive others.

Write Matthew 6:14-15 below. As you do, read the words aloud. Note the word "But."

_____

_____

_____

Now read Ephesians 4:31-32. What parallel do you see between this passage and Matthew 6:12,14-15?

_____

_____

_____

Look at Colossians 3:12-13. This passage on forgiveness gives us another view into what we are forgiving. What is it?

_____

_____

Peter asked Jesus, "How often shall my brother sin against me and I forgive him?" (Matt. 18:21). In Jesus' answer you will find your answer on the necessity of forgiveness. I've printed Matthew 18:21-35 so we can observe the same translation and not miss a thing.

Underline or color in red all references to _forgive_ and _forgave_.

21 _"Then Peter came and said to Him, 'Lord, how often shall my brother sin against me and I forgive him? Up to seven times?'_

22 _Jesus said to him, 'I do not say to you, up to seven times, but up to seventy times seven._

23 _For this reason the kingdom of heaven may be compared to a king who wished to settle accounts with his slaves._

24 _When he had begun to settle them, one who owed him ten thousand talents was brought to him._

25 _But since he did not have the means to repay, his lord commanded him to be sold, along with his wife and children and all that he had, and repayment to be made._

26 _So the slave fell to the ground and prostrated himself before him, saying, 'Have patience with me and I will repay you everything.'_

27 _And the lord of that slave felt compassion and released him and forgave him the debt._

28 _But that slave went out and found one of his fellow slaves who owed him a hundred denarii; and he seized him and began to choke him, saying, 'Pay back what you owe.'_

29 _So his fellow slave fell to the ground and began to plead with him, saying, 'Have patience with me and I will repay you.'_

30 _But he was unwilling and went and threw him in prison until he should pay back what was owed._

31 *So when his fellow slaves saw what had happened, they were deeply grieved and came and reported to their lord all that had happened.*

32 *Then summoning him, his lord said to him, 'You wicked slave, I forgave you all that debt because you pleaded with me.*

33 *Should you not also have had mercy on your fellow slave, in the same way that I had mercy on you?'*

34 *And his lord, moved with anger, handed him over to the torturers until he should repay all that was owed him.*

35 *My heavenly Father will also do the same to you, if each of you does not forgive his brother from your heart"* (Matt. 18:21-35).

What did you learn from marking the references to forgiving?

_____

_____

• **According to verse 35, what is the bottom line of this story of the king and the two slaves? And who is bottom-lining it?**

_____

_____

• **What is God's word to you?**

_____

_____

• **From what you have seen in God's Word, is there any way to get around forgiveness? (Remember Matt. 6:14-15.)**

_____

Now listen carefully, beloved. When you forgive someone, you are not releasing him or her from God's just punishment. Only God can do that. To obtain forgiveness they must believe on the Lord Jesus Christ, just as we had to do; otherwise, there is no forgiveness of their sins. If they do not believe, they will be judged according to their deeds, all which are written in the books (Matt. 25:41,46; Rev. 20:11-15).

God will deal justly with all who sin. But that is God's business, not yours. Yours is to forgive.

Have you seen, dear one, that forgiving others is a response of faith, an act of obedience? Obedience is not always easy; yet, you forgive because God tells you to forgive. It may not seem humanly reasonable or even emotionally possible. Although you do not feel a thing, you step out in faith's obedience because God says it.

Forgiveness is not a matter of feeling, of emotion; rather, it is an act of your will. Forgiveness is your response to God, not to your fellow man. Your transgressor may not deserve it, desire it, or require it; yet you forgive because God says to forgive. To not forgive is to disobey God and thus to sin. When you sin and do not repent, you invite the discipline of your Heavenly Father because a holy God must deal with sin.

To not forgive is not only to sin but it is also self-destructive. It will cannibalize your soul, eat you up from the inside out. An unwillingness to forgive leads to a root of bitterness that causes trouble and defiles many (Heb. 12:14-15). However, when you forgive—when you send away their debt—you'll find yourself released from the torturers.

I could tell you story after story of what happened when people were willing to forgive, but time and space do not permit my doing so. Just remember, the entire kingdom of God is comprised of people who have been forgiven their sin and reconciled to God. And it all happened when we were still enemies: "While we were enemies, we were reconciled to God" (Rom. 5:10).

Beloved, do you see it? There is no human being in the kingdom of God who is not a sinner, who has not offended our holy God, transgressed against Him, and yet who has not been forgiven by God and reconciled to Him through believing in the death, burial, and resurrection of Jesus Christ. Think, beloved. If a God who never sinned has forgiven us, how can we, as sinners, refuse to forgive one another?

IT'S TIME TO PRAY

"Forgive us ... as we also have forgiven." It's time to ask God if you need to forgive someone. Does anyone owe you a debt that you need to cancel? You've read His words. If you want forgiveness from your Heavenly Father, then you must forgive.

Talk to your Heavenly Father about it, and remember you've already prayed, "Your will be done, on earth as it is in heaven."

On a page you can place in your Bible list the names of those you need to forgive and why. Next to each name write: "On this date (and record the date) I chose to forgive you."

DAY 3 | **The Heart of an Intercessor**

REVIVAL! It's a familiar word in church circles. Revivals are advertised on the sign in front of the church informing all who are passing by of what is happening in the future. Or the sign heralds a "truth" needed for the week.

Revival is the plea of many a fervent spirit in private and in public prayer, "Oh God, have mercy, send revival." It is a divine moving of God that brings contrition at the price of personal pride.

Revival is a humbling of our souls that causes us to do away with sin and to live righteously in the midst of a crooked and perverse generation. It is an abhorrence of sin and a craving of righteousness. Revival is a divine move of God.

The one common denominator of all revivals is the acute awareness of sin and a cry for God's mercy. It is an awful consciousness of the awful holiness and purity of God that causes one to agonize over sin. It's a burning desire to confess all transgressions and be right with God, to seek reconciliation that you once refused to consider, to make restitution whatever the cost. Revival begins with the church and then moves to the streets bringing the worst of reprobates to their knees for salvation.

For the past two days we have dealt with the issue of sin on an individual level—the personal confession of sin and the need to forgive, but we have not yet touched the "us" that Jesus included in the way to pray: "Forgive us our debts, as we also have forgiven our debtors." This index sentence also is dealing with the *us,* the *our:* the acknowledgment of corporate sin and failure, of transgression and lawlessness, of compromise and complacency in respect to what God has said and ordered that can move us into revival as a church.

How desperately we need it! Pollsters tell us that those who profess to believe in the Lord Jesus Christ more closely resemble the world than their Lord. If all members of the body of Christ would allow themselves to be cleansed with the washing of the water of the Word, if everyone would pursue peace with all men and holiness (sanctification) as Hebrews 12:14 says, then there would be no need for corporate revival and the world would not shout "hypocrite!" They would either hate us or be converted because they would see an uncompromising love for God.

Sin is contagious. It spreads like a virus. The Bible likens sin to leaven that permeates the entire lump of dough. When it's not dealt with in the body of Christ, it ruins the spiritual health of the church and calls for God's judgment. If we won't judge sin in ourselves, then God must. This, I believe, is why Jesus included the "us" when it comes to asking forgiveness of our sins.

Are you familiar with Paul's words in 1 Corinthians 5:6-8 where he called the church to account for their arrogance in not dealing with sin in the church? For tolerating it? How could they who have been saved from sin condone sin in the body of Christ?

Look up 1 Corinthians 5:6-8 in your Bible. I want you to know what side of the page these verses are on so you can find them when you need them. For our purposes, they are printed below. Read the verses again, aloud, and do the following:

• Mark the reference to Passover with a red half circle like this: ⌒

• Underline each place "leaven" is used, and then list what you observe from the references to leaven in these verses.

> 6 *"Your boasting is not good. Do you not know that a little leaven leavens the whole lump of dough?*
> 7 *Clean out the old leaven so that you may be a new lump, just as you are in fact unleavened. For Christ our Passover also has been sacrificed.*
> 8 *Therefore, let us celebrate the feast, not with old leaven, nor with the leaven of malice and wickedness, but with the unleavened bread of sincerity and truth"* (1 Cor. 5:6-8).

_____

_____

• The reason for getting rid of the leaven is because Christ our Passover has been sacrificed. Why was Christ sacrificed? (If you don't know the answer, look at John 1:29.)

_____

_____

• So how are we as children of God to celebrate "the feast" (a picture of what Jesus accomplished for us in His death, keeping us from the wages of sin, which is death)?

_____

_____

_____

Are you celebrating the feast, beloved, by living according to truth rather than the Devil's lie? Are you sincere—the real thing? *Sincere* comes from two words: *sin* (without) and *cera* (wax). This word was put on fine china to indicate there were no cracks in the china that were covered by wax and fired in the kiln. (The cracks could be seen by holding the china up to the light of the sun.)

In Ezekiel 9, God was getting ready to send His destroyers in judgment on His rebellious city Jerusalem. However, before doing so, He called for a man with a writing case to go through the city and mark the forehead of all those "who sigh and groan over all the abominations which are being committed in its midst" (Ezek. 9:4). These are the ones who will be protected when God's rod of judgment falls on a land that "is filled with blood and … perversion" (v. 9). They are the ones who abhor sin and grieve over the condition of God's chosen people. And what of the others? "My eye will have no pity nor will I spare, but I will bring their conduct upon their heads" (v. 10).

It is time, beloved, to sigh and groan, to let our hearts be broken with the things that break God's heart. So let's look at the aspect of prayer—the "forgive us our sin"—that deals with corporate sin, the collective sin holding sway in the body of Christ. You can examine two different passages, one in Ezra and another in Daniel. Chronologically, Daniel precedes Ezra. Daniel spoke from captivity in Babylon while Ezra dealt with the remnant who later left Babylon to return to Jerusalem and rebuild the temple.

> **Choose one of the passages: Daniel 9:1-22 or Ezra 9:1-10. As you read, note how God is approached in prayer.**
>
> • **What is the attitude, the heart, of the intercessor?**
>
> _____
>
> _____
>
> • **Mark every reference to sin** (*iniquity, transgression, wickedness, rebelled, turned aside from Your commandments*). **Don't miss a synonym or any specified sin as mentioned in Ezra. (If you choose to study Ezra, please check out Deuteronomy 7:1-6.)**
>
> • **List what you learn from marking the references to sin.**
>
> _____
>
> _____
>
> • **What happened as a result of the intercession?**
>
> _____
>
> _____

In light of what you have seen today, what can you apply to your prayer life in the role of intercession? Write it down, and then we will put it into practice.

_____

_____

_____

_____

_____

IT'S TIME TO PRAY

Sit quietly before the Lord and reflect on the condition of the church to which you belong and on Christianity in general in our nation. How do we fall short of God's standard of righteousness? What are our "collective" or "corporate" sins? Certainly, materialism is one and immorality is another. What about being too busy to study God's Word, and as a result unable to handle the challenges we face?

Write down what comes to mind and keep the list in your Bible. Add to it as God continues to show you the condition of the church and a nation that once honored Him.

Considering what you learned from Daniel or Ezra, step into their roles on behalf of what you see.

- Begin by acknowledging the character and righteousness of God and His desire for His people to "be holy even as I am holy."
- Confess the sins of the people. Let your heart be broken with the things that break God's heart. If you studied the Daniel passage, you saw Daniel include himself as he confessed the shortcomings of Israel.
- Ask God to show you how to plead with Him on behalf of His people. Ask Him to move by His Spirit upon the hearts of people, to revive them, and to be merciful and compassionate to them.

DAY 4 | **Guard Duty for the Body**

How I will miss studying His Word with you! I know, beloved, that if you have done your homework, if you have given yourself to the disciplined study of His Word with a heart to hear and obey truth, that God has done a wonderful work within you. I also know that if you will continue to discipline yourself to discover truth for yourself and live in the light of it, God will bring you to an even greater maturity and usefulness in His kingdom.

That usefulness in His kingdom will be realized in part as you pray according to the sixth index or topical sentence of prayer: "And do not lead us into temptation, but deliver us from evil." It could also be translated "from the Evil One." It is the Evil One, the prince of this world and of the power of the air, the murderer, the liar and father of lies, the one who does not abide in truth, the tempter, the deceiver, the accuser of the brethren who reigns over evil.

Jesus' use of plural pronouns as He taught us to "pray in this way" makes it very clear that while the pray-er is included in the various topics of prayer, it is not just "all about me." When you and I believe on the Lord Jesus Christ and become children of God, we are placed into the body of Christ. As Ephesians teaches, we become part of the church, where the proper function of every member is critical to the health of His body. Thus, this aspect of prayer for us not to be led into temptation but delivered from evil is crucial. This is where we exercise vigilance. This is where God puts us on guard duty.

As we begin our look at this final topic, you need to know that some have problems with the fact that we would even have to say to God, "Do not lead us into temptation." James 1:13-14 says, "Let no one say when he is tempted, 'I am being tempted by God'; for God cannot be tempted by evil, and He Himself does not tempt anyone. But each one is tempted when he is carried away and enticed by his own lust." Therefore, since Scripture cannot contradict Scripture, it is obvious that we are not petitioning God not to tempt us, to solicit us to do evil. God cannot act in unrighteousness. So what is it saying?

Let me go into a little detail that I believe with give you the answer you are looking for. As I do, hang on; I need to get technical. It's OK to be stretched!

- "Lead," in the Greek, is *eispher*, which means "to bring to." It is an aorist active subjunctive verb.
- The aorist tense denotes punctilious action, occurring at one particular time.
- The active voice indicates that the subject produces the action of the verb. Therefore, it is God who brings or does not bring us into temptation.
- The subjunctive mood is a mood of probability and expresses an action that may or should happen but that is not necessarily true at present.

Therefore, the statement, "Do not lead us into temptation," is saying, in essence, "God, I am asking You not to bring us into temptation at any point in time."

Now, before you lean back in unbelief that God would ever bring us "into temptation," let's look at the word translated *temptation*. Then we will put it together in a practical way. The Greek word is *peirasmos* and is used for trials of varied character: trials, testings, temptations. Thus the word *peirasmos* must be interpreted according to its context. For instance, in James 1:2,12 *peirasmos* describes a trial we are to rejoice in, while in James 1:13-14 the same root word is used in connection with sin and is a temptation to be avoided.

What then is Matthew 6:13 saying? Well, we know it is not saying, "God, don't lead me into sin," because that is contrary to the character of God. And it contradicts James 1:13, "Let no one say when he is tempted, 'I am being tempted by God'; for God cannot be tempted by evil, and He Himself does not tempt anyone." What then is Jesus calling us to cover in prayer?

I believe this index sentence is a reminder or a call to vigilance in "preventive" prayer. When you come to this final topic of prayer, you are letting God know that your heart is set on righteousness, that you do not want to fail, to fall. When you find yourself in a trial *(peirasmos)*, if you do not count it all joy (Jas. 1:2), you are often tempted to give way to your flesh. If you do not realize that "the testing of your faith produces endurance" and you do not "let endurance have its perfect result, so that you may be perfect and complete, lacking in nothing" (Jas. 1:3-4), then you are liable to respond improperly in that trial, fall prey to the Evil One, and yield to temptation.

Let me give you an very ordinary illustration to which we all can relate. Jack and I had to be in Atlanta for a 12:30 p.m. appointment. Therefore, because it is a two-hour trip, we had to leave Chattanooga at 10:30 a.m. At 10:25 Jack walked out the door to go to the office, which is on the grounds where we live. Panicking, I ran after him to tell him we had to leave in five minutes.

At 10:35 I poured my sweet husband some coffee for the trip. At 10:45 I called the office in desperation, only to find that he had gone to the bank. To put it bluntly, I was flat-out angry. The coffee was cold, and so was I! By 11:00 I was so angry I could have cried. I had so carefully planned my morning for an on-time getaway, and now my plans were going up in smoke. I sat and tried to read a book on prayer, but concentration was impossible.

At 11:05 I heard a horn honk. As I walked out the door, mouth firmly set in displeasure, James 1:2-3 came to my mind: "Consider it all joy … trials … produces endurance." I got in the car, started to be ugly, but decided instead to walk by the Spirit and not fulfill the desire of my flesh. Our trip was only sweet because I decided in my trial, my *peirasmo*, to reign in my flesh by yielding to the Spirit whose fruit is love, joy, peace, and self-control! Which one of you was praying for me? How I appreciate it!

Can you begin to see how this index sentence on deliverance works? "Do not lead us into temptation, but deliver us from evil." We are telling God we do not want to be caught in the Devil's snare. This is preventive prayer, solicited and heard by our Father. And who do you think brought that Scripture to my mind as I walked out the door?

Let me give you another outstanding and helpful passage that parallels this index sentence on deliverance: Matthew 26:36-46. Let's return to the garden of Gethsemane. Read this passage carefully and then answer the questions that follow. Don't be tempted and go any further until you do this, beloved. Don't miss the joy of discovering truth for yourself!

> **As you read from your Bible, note or mark any references to "watching" and "praying."**

> • **What is the cup Jesus wanted His Father to remove? Compare this with John 18:11 and record your answer.**

> _____

> _____

> • **What do you learn from noting or marking the references to watching and praying?**

> _____

> _____

> • **List any parallel(s) between this prayer and the Lord's Prayer.**

> _____

> _____

> _____

To me, Matthew 26:41, "Keep watching and praying, that you may not enter into temptation," is almost an exact reiteration of what we are to pray in the Lord's Prayer. It is an acknowledgment that our flesh is weak even though our spirit is willing. It is an awareness of our utter dependence on God and our utter impotence against temptation apart from Him. Even Jesus asked three of His disciples to "keep watch with Him" (vv. 38,40).

And what happened to Peter? He slept. He did not watch and pray! Consequently, he would deny Jesus because he forgot his adversary, the Devil, was prowling about as a roaring lion seeking someone to devour (1 Pet. 5:8). Jesus had already told Peter that Satan desired to sift him as wheat and that He prayed for him (Luke 22:31-32). And yet Peter was not vigilant. Ultimately, Peter won the battle; his faith did not fail. He was not rendered impotent after his denial but was used of God to strengthen the brethren, yet he experienced bitter weeping (v. 62).

This final petition for deliverance in the Lord's instructions on the way to pray is an acknowledgment of the reality of spiritual warfare. Aware that Satan desires to sift us as wheat, even as he did Peter (v. 31), we are telling God that we realize we cannot handle the Evil One alone. We are willing to stand in righteousness, but God must do the delivering.

Oh, how you and I need to see this truth! Deliverance is always available for those who truly want it. Jesus will not have us pray a prayer that God will not answer! No Christian can ever say, "The Devil made me do it!" We have the promise of 1 Corinthians 10:13: "No temptation (*peirasmos*) has overtaken you but such as is common to man; and God is faithful, who will not allow you to be tempted beyond what you are able, but with the temptation will provide the way of escape also, so that you will be able to endure it."

Our final prayer is a prayer for deliverance. It is a cry to God out of poverty of spirit (Matt. 5:3), out of grief for falling short of His standard of holiness (v. 4), out of meekness (v. 5), out of a hunger and thirst for righteousness (v. 6), and out of purity of heart (v. 8). It is a cry that prays, "Spare me, Father, from needless trials or testings in which I might find myself tempted." Its cry acknowledges the reality of the Evil One and the Christian's warfare. It acknowledges that the flesh is weak. And last but not least, it heeds our Lord's admonition to "keep watching and praying that you may not enter into temptation; the spirit is willing, but the flesh is weak" (Matt. 26:41).

IT'S TIME TO PRAY

Today I want us to focus on ourselves. Like the flight attendant says when giving instructions for take-off, put the oxygen mask on yourself first so you can help those who need your assistance. You and I need to be kept from temptation so we will be on "praying ground," as the saying goes, and can intercede for others—a subject we will talk more about tomorrow.

Sit quietly before the Lord and ask Him to remind you of areas in which you are most vulnerable. Turn each of these areas into a matter of prayer. Ask God to deliver you from situations in which you might be tempted. Verbally affirm your hunger and thirst for righteousness, your desire for purity of heart.

Tell God you want to "be of sober spirit, be on the alert" for you know "your adversary, the devil, prowls around like a roaring lion, seeking someone to devour" and you want "to resist him, firm in your faith" (1 Pet. 5:8-9).

When you finish, thank God for hearing your prayer. Remember His promise that if we abide in Him and His words abide in us we can ask whatever we wish and it will be done (John 15:7).

DAY 5 | **Our Hallelujah of Worship**

We are to resist the Devil and remain firm in our faith. One way we can do so is through prayer—vigilant, preventive prayer for ourselves and our brothers and sisters in Christ. Their welfare, their steadfast endurance, impacts the entire body of Jesus Christ. What a high calling we have in this arena of prayer.

As I write this, I think of a missionary in Africa who awoke to find a strange man at the foot of her bed. His intention clearly was to assault her. Although frightened, a calmness came over her and her first impulse was to ask God what to do. She felt she was to show no fear but to rebuke him and command him to leave, which she did. Shocked, the man looked at her and fled.

Not too long after that the missionary received a letter from one of her supporters telling her that she had been awakened in the night to pray for her protection and wisdom. Immediately the intercessor went to her knees and stayed there until she had peace. She had stood guard in prayer, and the missionary had been delivered from the Evil One. When the missionary looked at the time of her intercessor's prayer, she realized that she had been on her knees before and during the man's appearance at the foot of her bed.

Such events happen over and over again. It is part of the mystery of the power of prayer, and you and I, beloved, can be part of these wonderful tales of deliverance if we will stand guard in prayer as faithful intercessors.

Let's look now at some references to prayer and to deliverance in the Word of God so we can see practically how all this works. It not only will bless you it also will equip you to give yourself to prayer.

> **Paul knew the power of vigilance in prayer. Read the following passages and ...**
> • **Mark any references to prayer as you've done previously.**
> • **Note what is being requested and underline it.**
> • **Circle the reason for the request if it is stated.**
> • **Write any personal insight or truth you want to remember.**
> • **If you have time, mark the same references in your Bible.**

> 30 *"Now I urge you, brethren, by our Lord Jesus Christ and by the love of the Spirit, to strive together with me in your prayers to God for me,*
> 31 *that I may be rescued from those who are disobedient in Judea, and that my service for Jerusalem may prove acceptable to the saints;*
> 32 *so that I may come to you in joy by the will of God and find refreshing rest in your company" (Rom. 15:30-32).*

_____

_____

8 *"For we do not want you to be unaware, brethren, of our affliction which came to us in Asia, that we were burdened excessively, beyond our strength, so that we despaired even of life;*

9 *indeed, we had the sentence of death within ourselves so that we would not trust in ourselves, but in God who raises the dead;*

10 *who delivered us from so great a peril of death, and will deliver us, He on whom we have set our hope. And He will yet deliver us,*

11 *you also joining in helping us through your prayers, so that thanks may be given by many persons on our behalf for the favor bestowed on us through the prayers of many"* (2 Cor. 1:8-11).

_____

_____

_____

_____

18 *"With all prayer and petition pray at all times in the Spirit, and with this in view, be on the alert with all perseverance and petition for all the saints,*

19 *and pray on my behalf, that utterance may be given to me in the opening of my mouth, to make known with boldness the mystery of the gospel,*

20 *for which I am an ambassador in chains; that in proclaiming it I may speak boldly, as I ought to speak"* (Eph. 6:18-20).

_____

_____

_____

_____

15 *"Some, to be sure, are preaching Christ even from envy and strife, but some also from goodwill*

16 *the latter do it out of love, knowing that I am appointed for the defense of the gospel;*

17 *the former proclaim Christ out of selfish ambition rather than from pure motives, thinking to cause me distress in my imprisonment.*

18 *What then? Only that in every way, whether in pretense or in truth, Christ is proclaimed; and in this I rejoice. Yes, and I will rejoice,*

19 *for I know that this will turn out for my deliverance through your prayers and the provision of the Spirit of Jesus Christ,*

20 *according to my earnest expectation and hope, that I will not be put to shame in anything, but that with all boldness, Christ will even now, as always, be exalted in my body, whether by life or by death" (Phil. 1:15-20).*

_____

_____

_____

1 *"Finally, brethren, pray for us that the word of the Lord will spread rapidly and be glorified, just as it did also with you;*

2 *and that we will be rescued from perverse and evil men; for not all have faith.*

3 *But the Lord is faithful, and He will strengthen and protect you from the evil one" (2 Thess. 3:1-3).*

_____

_____

_____

_____

Now consider what Paul urged us to pray for in these verses and think of how this would fit in the category of vigilance—deliverance from evil. As you do, think of what you hear and read in the news and the attacks in various countries, including the United States of America, against Christianity. "First of all, then, I urge that entreaties and prayers, petitions and thanksgivings, be made on behalf of all men, for kings and all who are in authority, so that we may lead a tranquil and quiet life in all godliness and dignity. This is good and acceptable in the sight of God our Savior, who desires all men to be saved and to come to the knowledge of the truth" (1 Tim. 2:1-4).

Precept Ministries International works in 149 countries and in 69 languages through the nationals we have trained in these countries. They are people of dedication and great passion, absolutely convinced that each person, young or old, should know how "to discover truth for yourself." Each has counted all things as loss so that others might know their God through studying His Word inductively. In order to accomplish this, many lay their freedom and their lives on the line day after day.

Sometimes I am overwhelmed by their sacrifice and circumstances. I think, *What can I do? How can I help?* It doesn't seem like much to say "I can pray" until I do a study like this and see the importance of vigilance in praying for the deliverance of my brothers and sisters and for the authorities over those countries. Then I begin to comprehend the vital, critical, protective role and power you and I have in prayer.

To pray this way is to pray our way to victory, for this aspect of prayer says, "I know that we—my brothers and sisters and I—are in a warfare, and we will to persevere, to be faithful unto death. We choose to win—and win we shall with the help of each other's prayers and the power of the Spirit of God." Surely those who pray this way are "on the alert with all perseverance and petition for all the saints" (Eph. 6:18), and Jesus our Teacher is pleased.

Although the last sentence of Jesus' instruction in prayer, "For Yours is the kingdom and the power and the glory forever. Amen," is not in the earliest manuscripts, is it any wonder that it was added as a hallelujah of triumph, of worship? It makes the seventh index sentence—and seven is the number of perfection—give this prayer a sense of completeness.

Oh, beloved, pause a minute. Hush! Listen! Can you not hear the hallelujahs from heaven? "Thanks be to God, who always leads us in triumph in Christ" (2 Cor. 2:14)! Here we have the perfect way to pray, taught to us by the One who ever lives to make intercession for the children of God. We know how to pray, don't we, beloved! We know what to pray!

> "*Pray, then, in this way: 'Our Father who is in heaven, Hallowed be Your name. Your kingdom come. Your will be done, On earth as it is in heaven. Give us this day our daily bread. And forgive us our debts, as we also have forgiven our debtors. And do not lead us into temptation, but deliver us from evil. For Yours is the kingdom and the power and the glory forever. Amen'*" (Matt. 6:9-13).

IT'S TIME TO PRAY

I don't think anything would be more fitting than to close our study in watching and praying for the body of Christ, by taking the truths we learned these past two days and putting them into practice. For whom can we specifically pray?

Ask your Father to show you those He wants you to intercede for today, that they would be delivered from evil and the Evil One. As you pray, remember, dear one, His is the kingdom and the power and the glory forever and ever and ever. We win because He has already won. He watched and prayed and said, "Not My will, but Yours be done" (Luke 22:42).

WEEKENDER

Learning to pray God's way according to His Word becomes a pattern when we spend time with Him every day. Each week a Weekender page helps you include time with Him in your weekend schedule, As you refresh from the week, don't miss a day in the Word and in communication with the Father.

What power is God revealing in the world as you practice the Lord's Prayer?

_____

_____

_____

_____

_____

How has God been answering your prayers this week?

_____

_____

_____

_____

_____

STAYING IN THE WORD

SESSION 5 • STAYING IN THE WORD

Index Sentence 5: "Forgive us our debts, as we also have forgiven our debtors."

I am asking God to forgive me to the _extent_ that I have forgiven others.

The kingdom of God is all about _forgiveness_ _of_ _sins_

and _restoration_ .

Prayer is _approaching_ _our_ _father_ who is in heaven.

Who can approach Him this way? Someone who has:
Clean hands
A pure heart
Honesty and integrity

God is a holy God and we must treat Him as _holy_ .

The more you're in the Word of God, the more you will be clean.

"Do you not know that friendship with the world is hostility toward God? Therefore whoever wishes to be a friend of the world makes himself an enemy of God" (Jas. 4:4).

We belong to him , not to the world.

It is so important that we _stay in the word_ of God.

Index Sentences 6 and 7: "Do not lead us into temptation, but deliver us from evil. For Yours is the kingdom and the power and the glory forever. Amen."

Precautionary prayer: We _beseech_ God.

Luke 22:31-32: "strengthen your brothers" (v. 32).

This is God's way to pray.

James 4:5-10

NOTES

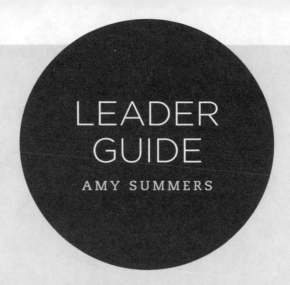

LEADER GUIDE

AMY SUMMERS

Congratulations on being called to lead a small-group discussion for *Lord, Teach Me to Pray: Practicing a Powerful Pattern of Prayer*. You will be doubly blessed as you not only delve into God's Word and learn to pray yourself but also guide other women through this study. This leader guide will help you facilitate five 1½ hour group sessions.

Session 1, as an introductory session, will be a time for women to receive their copies of *Lord, Teach Me to Pray*, get to know one another, and familiarize themselves with the workbook and Kay through her introductory video.

We recommend you purchase the DVD available in the Leader Kit (Item 1-4158-3212-9). If you do not use the DVD, you may choose not to have an introductory session, but make certain participants have their books in time to complete week 1 before your first session.

Each session's leader guide is divided into five main segments. You may revise these ideas to fit the needs of the group, but make certain that the elements of discussion, application, and praying are included. If you have more or less than 1½ hours for each session, then adjust the time suggestions accordingly.

1. **Build** is a time for welcome, quick announcements, and an activity that introduces the session and helps participants become comfortable with one another. As hard as it may be to start sessions on time—do so! Those who are chattering will stop, and those who are chronically late will begin to come earlier if they realize they are missing something! *(5 min. suggested)*
2. **Discuss** helps you guide women to discuss what they learned in their personal Bible study the past week. Emphasize to the women the extreme importance of doing their own study. You cannot cover all the rich treasures that Kay has presented in days 1-5 of each week in this short discussion time. However, the **Discuss** segment will help participants further understand what they have already discovered on their own. *(30 min. suggested)*
3. **View** Kay's teaching. *(approximately 30 min. per video session)*
4. **Apply** guides participants to explore how their personal study, the group's discussion, and Kay's teaching have worked together to help them begin to accomplish the week's goals listed on the first page of each week of study. *(10 min. suggested)*

5. **Pray** guides women to practice what they have learned about prayer by actually praying. This is not a time for prayer requests unless specifically directed! God knows what we need before we ask Him (Matt. 6:8), so you don't need to feel you are neglecting women's needs by not discussing and praying for those requests. If you desire the group to pray about specific needs for one another, enlist someone to coordinate a prayer chain or invite women to stay for an additional prayer time after your session has ended. Use this **Pray** time to apply the principles of prayer that were discussed in the week's study and video. *(15 min. suggested)*

For most sessions, your main preparation is to cue the video in advance. **Before the Session** indicates special instructions for sessions 1 and 5. If you are coming to the end of each session with little time to pray, then adjust your schedule. Spend less time on **Build, Discuss,** or **Apply**, but don't neglect to **Pray!**

Leading a Discussion Group

You don't need to be a gifted teacher, natural leader, or a powerful prayer warrior to facilitate these small-group sessions. What do you need?
- a hunger and thirst to connect with your Heavenly Father in an intimate way
- compassion for others who desperately desire to know God and have a powerful prayer life
- a monitor and DVD player
- childcare. Mothers need this uninterrupted time of study and discussion. Ask the Lord to provide childcare. Then rejoice when you see your first prayer for this study answered!
- a meeting place. If you plan to use this study as an outreach for non-churched women, then you might consider a location other than a church. (Remember, Kay's groups once met in a barn!) Make sure it's comfortable and large enough for women to sit in a circle and see clearly.

Ask God to put together the small groups He desires for this study. Groups of 12 or fewer are ideal for freely sharing thoughts and ideas. If you have more than 12 women, be sure to have them discuss some questions in smaller groups of three or four to ensure that the quieter women get a chance to talk.

Announce the study in your church newsletter, worship bulletin, and bulletin boards. Encourage women to invite any of their unchurched friends to participate. This study is for mature Christians, brand-new Christians, and it can also lead women to become Christians. How exciting!

Before each session, complete each week's assignments prayerfully and thoroughly. The most effective way you can lead this class is by allowing God's Word to transform you and then letting that transformation overflow to the women in your small group. Read through the leader guide suggestions for each session and adapt them to the needs of your group and the length of your sessions. After each session, evaluate the group experience.

Here's help to quickly locate where teaching *begins* on each index sentence: *Overview and index sentence 1 (worship)* begins on page 23; *index sentence 2 (allegiance)* begins on page 40; *index sentence 3 (submission)* begins on page 52; *index sentence 4 (petition and provision)* begins on page 75, *index sentence 5 (confession and forgiveness)* begins on page 93, *index sentence 6 (watchfulness and deliverance)* begins on page 105; *index sentence 7*, on page 112. (Of course, many overlap!)

SESSION 1 | **You Are God's Precious Creation**

Before the Session
1. Have copies of *Lord, Teach Me to Pray* ready for distribution. (See p. 2 for the ordering information.)
2. Prepare an attendance sheet for participants to indicate their names, addresses, phone numbers, and e-mail addresses. Place this on a table near the door with pens, markers, name tags, and a basket for collecting money if participants are paying for their member books. (A little basket with chocolates or mints would be nice as well!)
3. Read "About the Author," "About the Study," and "Introduction: Before You Begin." Be prepared to share your condensed version of this information.
4. Have the TV ready and the DVD cued to the session 1 video.

During the Session
BUILD (Take about 20 min. for this introductory **Build** time since **Discuss** will be shorter today.)
1. As women arrive, ask them to sign in, prepare name tags, and pick up copies of *Lord, Teach Me to Pray*. Invite them to leave payment for their books in the basket or offer to collect their money after the session.
2. Ask the women to introduce themselves to the group and to relate: (1) the most important human relationships in their lives, and (2) the person to whom they talk the most. As the leader, go first to get the ball rolling.
3. After all the women have introduced themselves, remark that it is obvious that relationships and communication are strongly interconnected. The women in this group will grow in their relationships with one another as they communicate in this study over the next five weeks. More importantly, they will grow in their relationship with the Heavenly Father as they communicate with Him through Bible study and prayer.
4. Use information from "About This Study" to assure the women they can and will learn how to pray if they faithfully apply themselves to this study.
DISCUSS (about 10 min. for today's session)
1. Ask the women to leaf through week 1 (pp. 10–34) and note the five-day and Weekender format of this study. Encourage them to study daily and to complete, in writing, every activity and prayer feature. Remind learners that

they will learn to pray only as they daily spend private time with Jesus and allow the Holy Spirit to teach them.

VIEW (about 30 min.)
1. Request women turn to the video listening guide on page 8 and take additional notes on page 9 as they watch the video.
2. Play the session 1 video.

APPLY (15 min.)
1. Allow women to share what was most meaningful to them from the video.
2. Ask women to state their goals for this study. Remark that Kay has listed goals for each week but admits that God's plans are so much higher than anyone can imagine. Ask a volunteer to read aloud Isaiah 55:8-9 and another to read 1 Corinthians 2:9.

PRAY (15 min.)
1. Explain that a vital part of each session will be a group prayer time. Tell the women you will give directions to guide each session's prayer time. Assure women that while they may find it beneficial to pray out loud, they do not have to do so.
2. Use Kay's video teaching outline on page 8 as the guide for today's prayer time. First, guide the women to pray one sentence, praising God for being holy and creating all things. Next, instruct them to thank God for giving us a book of prayer. Then guide them to ask God to help them learn how to approach Him as holy. Finally, instruct the women to pray together, "Lord, teach me to pray."
3. Use 1 Corinthians 2:9 as the basis for your final closing prayer, thanking God that no mind has conceived the marvelous things He has prepared for your small group through this study.

SESSION 2 | **Learning to Pray God's Way**

In advance cue the DVD to session 2.

During the Session
BUILD (5 min.)
1. Invite women to share their top two priorities for every day. Ask how their priorities determine all their other actions.
DISCUSS (30 min.)
Day 1
1. What were the top two priorities of the early church leaders and why?
2. What did you learn about the connection between prayer, God's Word, and your relationship with God from John 15:7 and 1 John 5:13-15?

Day 2

1. Who initiated the relationship between you and God? According to John 1:12, what is your responsibility and God's promise in this relationship?
2. Urge women to make certain they have a personal relationship with Jesus Christ. Invite women to share if they received Christ as a result of their study of day 2. If so, stop and praise God for bringing salvation to your group!
3. If you had been a disciple, which of the instances of observing Jesus praying in the Luke passages would have prompted you to ask Him to teach you to pray? Why?

Day 3

1. Why is the title of this study such a precious promise? Where must we begin if we really want to learn to pray?
2. What insights to prayer did you glean from Matthew 6:5-13?
3. What are index sentences or prayers?

Day 4

1. Identify the seven topics of prayer covered in the Lord's Prayer. How do these cover every one of your prayer needs?
2. Why is it significant that the Lord's Prayer begins with "Our Father?" (Draw from day 5 as well to explore this question.)

Day 5

1. Why does all true prayer begin with worship?
2. Contrast how believers hallow and hollow God's name.
3. Which name of God is the most meaningful to you at this point in your life? Why did you make this choice?
4. Based on what you discovered from Isaiah 37, 2 Chronicles 20, and Acts 4, what is the first thing we should do when life attacks us? Why?

VIEW (30 min.)

1. Request women turn to the viewer guide on page 34 and take additional notes on page 35 as they watch the video.
2. Play the session 2 video.

APPLY (10 min.)

1. Read the goals for week 1 on page 10. Invite women to share how their personal study, the group's discussion, and Kay's teaching have helped them begin to accomplish those goals.

PRAY (15 min.)

1. Lead the women in a time of worship by instructing them to choose a name of God from page 31 and praise Him for that character quality. For example, "God, I praise you because You are the Lord who is there" or "I worship you because You are the Creator and the Most High God."
2. Ask God to help each woman to 1) make prayer and His Word the top two priorities in her life and 2) begin and end her prayers and days with worship.

SESSION 3 | **It's All About Him**

In advance cue the DVD to session 3.

During the Session

BUILD (5 min.)

1. Invite volunteers to name every person in the small group. Ask the women if they are hesitant to speak with someone whose name they have forgotten and why. Inquire: How strong a relationship with someone can you have if you don't know their name or anything about their character? Why?

DISCUSS (30 min.)

Day 1

1. What does Kay mean by "rehearsing the character of God," and why is that vital for a powerful prayer life?
2. What was the most meaningful character quality you learned about God from the three biblical prayers you examined and why? What did you learn from these three figures about using your knowledge of God in prayer?

Day 2

1. Identify the second index sentence of the Lord's Prayer. What did you learn about God's kingdom from Matthew 28:18-20?
2. What does it mean to pledge allegiance to God's kingdom? What are the things to which many people give their allegiance? What effect does this have both on their relationships with God and on their prayer lives?
3. What kind of allegiance does Jesus want from us? How can we follow Jesus' example when Satan tries to tempt us to give him our allegiance instead?

Day 3

1. Based on the learning activities and Kay's remarks, what is our mission and commission as believers? What role does prayer play in accomplishing that mission? What impact should our mission have on the way we pray?

Day 4

1. What is the third index sentence of the Lord's Prayer? What heart attitude should this prayer indicate?
2. What did you discover about God's will from the passages in John?
3. Read Matthew 7:21-27 and follow Kay's reasoning questions to explore the relationship between submission, salvation, and answered prayers.

Day 5

1. Why could Jesus in all integrity teach us to pray "Your will be done"? What did you learn about submitting to God from Jesus' prayer in Matthew 26:36-44?
2. Can you be involved in seeing Jesus' kingdom come if you aren't willing to say "Your will be done"? Why?
3. Why did Paul want readers to be filled with knowledge of God's will (Col.1:9-12)?

VIEW (30 min.)

1. Request women turn to the viewer guide on page 62 and take additional notes on page 63 as they watch the video.
2. Play the session 3 video.

APPLY (10 min.)

1. Read the goals for week 2 on page 36. Invite women to share how their personal study, the group's discussion, and Kay's teaching have helped them begin to accomplish those goals.

PRAY (15 min.)

1. Instruct women to pray aloud Colossians 1:9-12 (p. 59), inserting the names of the persons they feel led to pray for in the place of "you" in the passage.
2. When all women have prayed, pray aloud Colossians 1:9-12 for the group, using "we" in place of "you."

SESSION 4 | **You Belong to God**

In advance cue the DVD to session 4.

During the Session
BUILD (5 min.)

1. Ask women to indicate if they've ever struggled to know the will of God in a matter. Ask why they think discerning God's will is difficult for so many Christians. Direct women to get into groups of three. Instruct them to share with their small group an area where they are seeking God's will. Encourage them to write one another's names and area of need to know God's will on the inside front cover of their workbook as a commitment to pray for one another throughout this study.

DISCUSS (30 min.)
Day 1

1. What's the change in focus from Matthew 6:9-10 and 11-13? What's the reason for that order of focus?
2. What did you learn about God's will from Romans 12:1-2?
3. How did George Mueller's example in this reading change the way you approach decision making?

Day 2

1. What do the personal pronouns in the Lord's Prayer indicate about prayer?
2. Based on all the Scriptures you explored, what do you think *intercession* means? Based on Revelation 1:5-6, what is our role in intercession?
3. How did you feel to discover that Jesus always lives to intercede for you? Why? How were you encouraged by Romans 8:26-27?

Day 3

1. What is the fourth index sentence? What topic does it cover?
2. Why did we need to delve into the subject of faith as we began to look at petition?
3. What did you learn about faith from Hebrews 11:1-3? How would you describe a faith that soars?

Day 4

1. When it comes to having your needs met, what is your responsibility according to all the verses we looked at in this day?
2. What does the handwriting of God tell us to do? What does He promise to do? How can you give personal testimony that He keeps His promises when it comes to supplying your needs?

Day 5

1. Identify the five principles of having our needs met.
2. What did you learn about prayer and the boundaries within God's Word from the Scripture activity on page 85?
3. What does it mean to plead the promises of God? What must we know before we can do that?
4. How did Luke 18:1-8 challenge and encourage you?

VIEW (30 min.)

1. Request women turn to the viewer guide on page 90 and take additional notes on page 91 as they watch the video.
2. Play the session 4 video.

APPLY (10 min.)

1. Read the goals for week 3 on page 64. Invite women to share how their personal study, the group's discussion, and Kay's teaching have helped them begin to accomplish those goals.

PRAY (15 min.)

1. Request women get back in the same groups of three from **Build.** Instruct them to share one specific need with one another and write those in the front of the book where they've already written each other's names. Instruct them to pray for one another in two areas: 1) discerning God's will in the situation they mentioned earlier; and 2) their specific need to be met according to God's will and timing. Encourage them to use Scriptures that are printed in this week's lesson in their prayers.
2. Read Ephesians 3:20-21 as your closing prayer of praise and faith.

SESSION 5 | **Staying in the Word**

Before the Session

1. Cue the DVD to session 5.
2. Write each of the seven index sentences of the Lord's Prayer (see p. 24) on small poster boards. Display these visuals on walls in your meeting space.
3. This session is different to allow more time for prayer. The **Build** and **Apply** times have been omitted, although building relationships and applying God's truths should occur naturally in your **Discuss** and **Pray** times.

During the Session
DISCUSS (30 min.)

Day 1
1. Identify the fifth index sentence in the Lord's Prayer.
2. Why aren't sin and forgiveness dealt with earlier in the prayer?
3. What did you learn about the relationship between sin and prayer from the verses on page 96?

Day 2
1. What was the most challenging truth you learned about forgiveness from your Scripture study?
2. Who do you really release when you forgive someone who has wronged you? Explain.
3. How is forgiving others ultimately a matter between you and God?

Day 3
1. Define *revival*. Why is revival necessary? What must happen for revival to occur?
2. What did you learn from Daniel's or Ezra's example that you can apply to your life as an intercessor?

Day 4
1. State the sixth index sentence in the Lord's Prayer. How does this prayer topic put us on guard duty for the body of Christ?
2. What similarities do you see between the sixth index sentence and Matt. 26:41?
3. Read 1 Corinthians 10:13. What is God's role and our responsibility in our not yielding to temptation?

Day 5
1. Can you share a testimony about the mystery of the power of prayer similar to the missionary's experience? How can we be part of this great mystery?
2. What insights into prayer did you gain from your study of the Scriptures?
3. How has this study made you more of a prayer warrior for our world?
4. Identify the seventh index sentence. How does it bring prayer full circle?

VIEW (30 minutes)
1. Request women turn to the video viewer guide on page 114 and take additional notes on page 115 as they watch the video.
2. Play the session 5 video.

PRAY (30 minutes)
1. Ask women to get into groups of two or three. Instruct groups to pray "around the room" by standing next to an index sentence displayed on the wall. The group should pray for five minutes on that topic and then move to another index sentence. Groups don't all need to begin with the first index sentence but may rotate in an orderly fashion. Encourage women to use the truths and Scriptures they have learned in this study as they pray each topic. Indicate when time is up so groups know to move to the next prayer station.
2. When all groups have prayed at all seven stations, gather everyone as a large group and pray (don't recite) together the Lord's Prayer.

BORN AGAIN

Have you ever wondered what the phrase "born again" means? The Bible records that Jesus used the phrase in a conversation with a man named Nicodemus who approached Jesus at night, curious about Jesus and what He had to say about the kingdom of God.

Jesus told Nicodemus, "Except a man be born again, he cannot see the kingdom of God" (John 3:3, KJV). Nicodemus responded, "How can a man be born when he is old?" (v. 4).

Nicodemus was a highly moral man who obeyed God's law. He was a respected leader of the Jewish community. No doubt he was a fine man. Yet something was lacking.

Like Nicodemus, many people today confuse religion with new birth in Christ. Phrases like "I pray regularly" or "I believe there is a God" often are confused with a real new-birth experience.

New birth begins with the Holy Spirit convicting a person of sin. Because of sin, we are spiritually dead. For this reason, spiritual birth, as Jesus described it, is necessary. God loves us and gives us spiritual birth when we ask Him for it.

The Bible says all persons are sinners (Romans 3:23). Jesus died on a cross and was raised from the dead to save sinners. To be born again means that a person admits to God that he or she is a sinner, repents of sin, believes in or trusts Christ, and confesses faith in Christ as Savior and Lord.

Jesus told Nicodemus that everyone who believes in (places faith in) Christ would not perish (John 3:16). Jesus is the only One who can save us (John 14:6). To believe in Jesus is to be born again. Confess your sins and ask Jesus right now to save you. "And it shall come to pass, that whosoever shall call on the name of the Lord shall be saved" (Acts 2:21, KJV).

After you have received Jesus Christ into your life, share your decision with another person, and following Christ's example, ask for baptism by immersion in your local church as a public expression of your faith (Rom. 6:4; Col. 2:6).

Knowing How to Pray Can Change Your Life

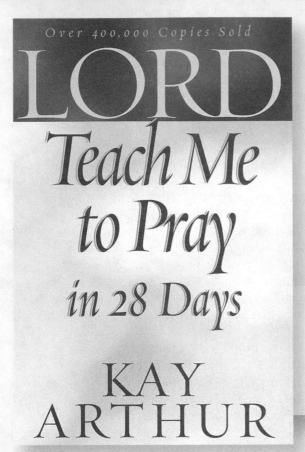

Over 400,000 Copies Sold

LORD
Teach Me to Pray
in 28 Days

KAY ARTHUR

Many books offer tips on enhancing your prayer life…but they leave you adrift when it comes to actually praying. In this 28-day study, Kay Arthur provides intensely practical insights to help you know *how* to pray, *what* to pray, and *what to expect* when you pray.

Thankfully, Jesus gave His disciples the perfect pattern for meaningful prayer. It is refreshingly simple and exceedingly powerful—and it can begin to transform the way you pray (and live) today!

"Every requirement for prayer, every element of worship and praise, every perspective of intercession and petition is covered in the Lord's prayer. What a treasure our Lord gave us!"

—**Kay Arthur**

Kay Arthur and her husband, Jack, are the founders of Precept Ministries International. This ministry reaches hundreds of thousands of people internationally through "Precept Upon Precept" Bible studies and Kay's radio and television program, *Precepts for Life*. Kay is the bestselling author of more than 100 books and Bible studies, and is also the active spokeswoman for *The New Inductive Study Bible*.

HARVEST HOUSE PUBLISHERS

To learn more about Kay Arthur or to read a sample chapter, visit:
www.HarvestHousePublishers.com

Phslippian 3

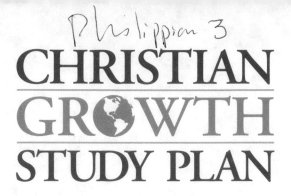

CHRISTIAN GROWTH STUDY PLAN

In the Christian Growth Study Plan (formerly Church Study Course), *Lord, Teach Me to Pray* is a resource for course credit in the subject area Bible Studies of the Christian Growth category of plans. To receive credit, read the book, complete the learning activities, show your work to your pastor, a staff member, or church leader, then complete the following information. This page may be duplicated. Send the completed page to:

Christian Growth Study Plan; One Life-Way Plaza; Nashville, TN 37234-0117; FAX: (615) 251-5067; E-mail: *cgspnet@lifeway.com*. For information about the Christian Growth Study Plan, refer to the Christian Growth Study Plan Catalog. It is located online at *www.lifeway.com/cgsp*. If you do not have access to the Internet, contact the Christian Growth Study Plan office at 1 (800) 968-5519 for the specific plan you need for your ministry.

Lord, Teach Me to Pray
Course Number: CG-1123

PARTICIPANT INFORMATION

Social Security Number (USA ONLY-optional)	Personal CGSP Number*	Date of Birth (MONTH, DAY, YEAR)
– –	– –	– –

Name (First, Middle, Last)		Home Phone
		– –

Address (Street, Route, or P.O. Box)	City, State, or Province	Zip/Postal Code

Email Address for CGSP use

Please check appropriate box: ❏ Resource purchased by church ❏ Resource purchased by self ❏ Other

CHURCH INFORMATION

Church Name

Address (Street, Route, or P.O. Box)	City, State, or Province	Zip/Postal Code

CHANGE REQUEST ONLY

☐ Former Name

☐ Former Address	City, State, or Province	Zip/Postal Code

☐ Former Church	City, State, or Province	Zip/Postal Code

Signature of Pastor, Conference Leader, or Other Church Leader	Date

*New participants are requested but not required to give SS# and date of birth. Existing participants, please give CGSP# when using SS# for the first time. Thereafter, only one ID# is required. **Mail to:** Christian Growth Study Plan, One LifeWay Plaza, Nashville, TN 37234-0117. Fax: (615)251-5067.

Revised 4-05